I0762226

TAMU

TAMU

A Journey Through Africa's Plant-Based Cuisine

Jane Nshuti

Photography by
Livhuwani Ravele

PRESTEL
MUNICH · LONDON · NEW YORK

CONTENTS

Introduction

When I was about eight years old, I asked my mama if I could make rice for my family, and she said yes. We were a family of six and I was the youngest; you can imagine my excitement when I was allowed to step into the kitchen to cook for all of us – under strict supervision, of course – and the end result was great. That rice was perfect!

Before that I had been watching my brother Leonard in the kitchen and by doing so, I slowly started developing a love of cooking. His homemade samosas and meatballs made him super popular in our neighbourhood, but it was his omelette-flipping skills that made me want to cook like him one day.

A year after my rice-cooking experience I found myself in a position where my cooking skills were really put to the test. Like many families from my home country Rwanda, my family has experienced great tragedy. My siblings and I lost our parents in 1994 during the turmoil in the country and became refugees in the Democratic Republic of Congo (DRC), then known as Zaire. My eldest sibling was 17 years old and I was only nine at the time. It was just the four of us against the world!

As we tried to survive and navigate through life in a refugee camp, my older siblings had to find ways to put food on our non-existent table. Since I was too young to join them in trying to make money and contribute to bringing food home, my duties were to help fetch water and to prepare something to eat with whatever they brought home.

This is where my creativity in the kitchen began. When I say we didn't have much, that would be putting it mildly. We were simply lucky if my siblings returned home with anything at all. Back then I didn't know much about cooking, but I quickly learnt that it's about following a concept and creating one's own interpretation – that's how real masterpieces are born. It was during this season in my life that I learnt the art of improvising and making do with whatever I had. I also started creating my own recipes using tips I had learnt from my late mama and from watching my siblings cook.

I hope this book sparks a passion for food in you. I want us to travel around Africa together and rediscover what food means and what food does for each of us. In Swahili, the word tamu means delicious, and that's exactly what I hope you find in these pages – a celebration of the rich, joyful and tamu flavours of African cuisine. I want us to celebrate African flavours, tell African stories and thank God for the land He has given us to plant and harvest. I pray that when all is said and done, your love of African food will be born, and I hope you connect to the continent through my cooking.

Before we take off, here is a recipe for a quick moringa latte you can sip on as we embark on this exciting journey.

Moringa Latte

MAKES 1

- 150 ml (2/3 cup) plant milk of your choice, heated
- 1 tsp moringa powder, plus extra for garnish
- 1 tsp agave syrup or any other sweetener of your choice

1. Gently heat the milk in a saucepan until warm but not boiling.
2. Pour 75 ml (1/3 cup) of the heated milk into a small jug. Use a hand milk frother to froth the milk until it develops a nice foam.
3. In a mug, combine the remaining milk with the moringa powder and agave syrup. Stir well until the moringa powder and agave syrup are fully dissolved.
4. Gently pour the frothed milk into the mug with the moringa mixture.
5. Sprinkle a dash of moringa powder on top for garnish.

NOTE:

- Adjust the sweetness or the amount of moringa to suit your taste.

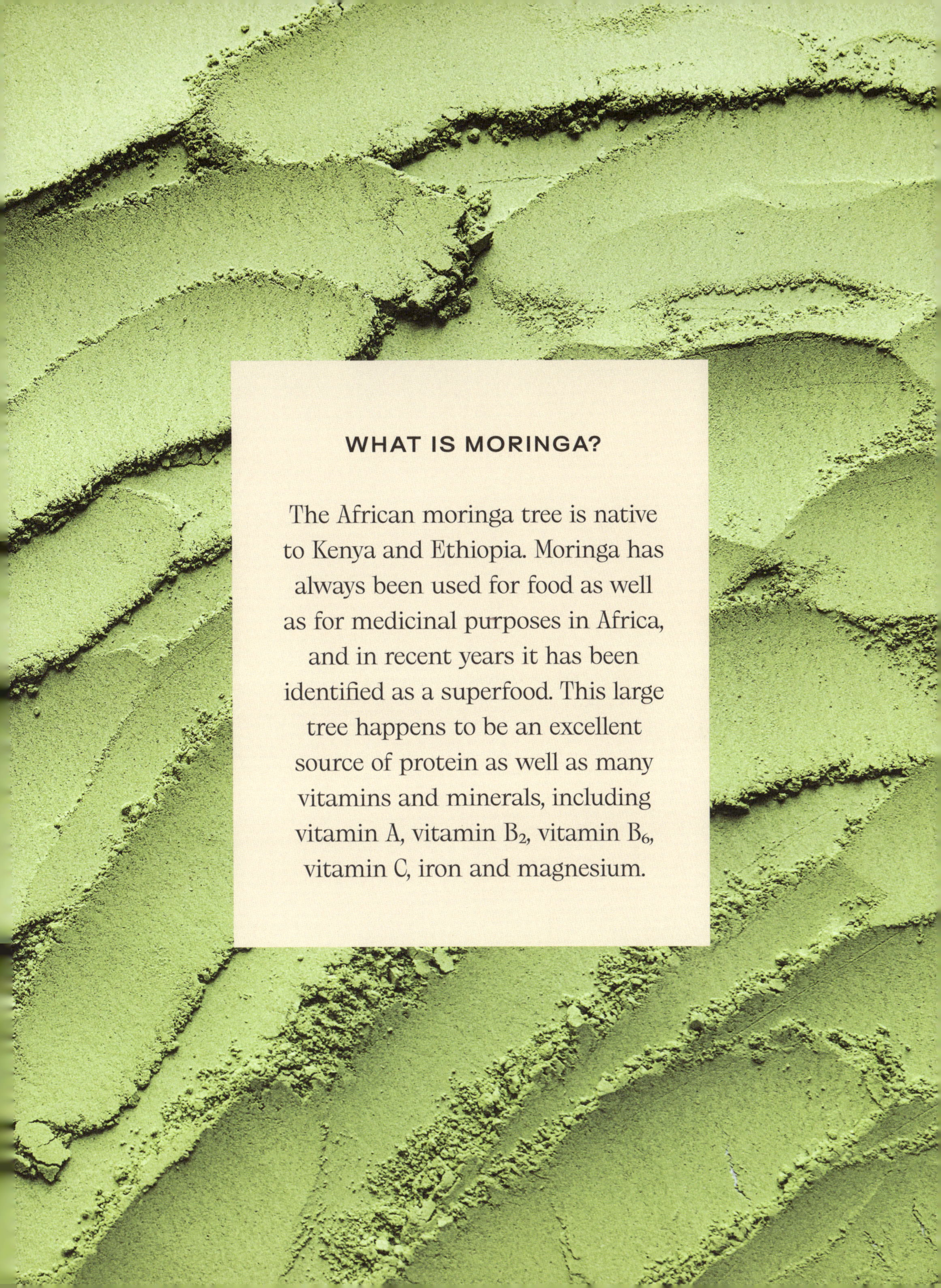

WHAT IS MORINGA?

The African moringa tree is native to Kenya and Ethiopia. Moringa has always been used for food as well as for medicinal purposes in Africa, and in recent years it has been identified as a superfood. This large tree happens to be an excellent source of protein as well as many vitamins and minerals, including vitamin A, vitamin B_2, vitamin B_6, vitamin C, iron and magnesium.

THE COUNTRIES I WRITE ABOUT

When I was very young, life took me on an unexpected journey that would change me forever. Like thousands of other Rwandans, I left Rwanda and found myself in the DRC. Two years later, one of my siblings and I set out on yet another life-changing journey to live with our uncle in Kenya. This wasn't a direct path; we first travelled to Uganda, where we stayed with a friend of my uncle's while waiting for him to come and take us to Kenya.

Finally, my uncle arrived. He and my aunt had taken in my brother and I as their own, giving us the chance to have them as parents, with their children becoming like siblings to us. We travelled with him to Kenya, where we lived with his family for four years. But life kept calling us onward. We journeyed through Tanzania, Malawi and Mozambique until we eventually arrived in South Africa.

In each country we became part of the community, connecting with people from all walks of life. If I wrote about every food experience from each place I've lived in or passed through, it would take a lifetime. Instead, I've chosen the memories that linger most vividly in my mind, leaving space for stories from African countries I haven't yet visited, but have heard great things about, especially in North and West Africa.

In this book I've given you a glimpse of my experiences in Rwanda, Kenya, Tanzania, South Africa and Mozambique, as well as the DRC and Uganda in passing. I've also shared the encounters I've had with people from Burkina Faso, Ghana, Nigeria, Zambia, Ethiopia, Morocco and Egypt. I hope that by journeying down memory lane with me, you'll feel inspired to experience these incredible places for yourself one day.

SETTING THE STAGE

Wherever you are on your cooking journey, this book invites you to discover, explore and embrace African flavours. Some ingredients may be unfamiliar to you or hard to find, but that's part of the adventure! Seek out local ethnic stores, experiment with new methods and feel free to add your own unique touch. Cooking, like any art, grows with curiosity and practice.

For me, cooking began out of responsibility, but as I travelled and experienced diverse cuisines it ignited a passion in me for the art of food. I was especially moved by the beauty of African flavours, which are often underappreciated. This journey showed me how food can be a powerful way to tell stories and connect cultures. I hope this book helps you to experience Africa's richness through her foods, to learn about different countries and to make new connections through the shared joy of cooking.

Join me on this flavourful ride around Africa, where we'll explore indigenous ingredients, connect through stories and celebrate the beauty of African cuisine.

GOING PLANT-BASED, AFRICAN STYLE

Cooking started off as more of a responsibility than a discovery for me. When we were in the refugee camp, I cooked out of duty instead of love. It was only later in life, when I was exposed to more foods from different countries that I was privileged to visit and live in, that a new kind of passion was ignited within me.

As my passion continued to grow and received more exposure, I was disappointed by how little the world knew about African food, and how African ingredients and flavours are often so underrated, unappreciated and inaccessible, even on the continent. It breaks my heart that I can find restaurants that make international dishes on every busy street in Cape Town and yet there are very few African cuisine restaurants.

There were times when I would eat out in restaurants simply so that I could imagine how dishes were prepared and how I could incorporate African ingredients into some of my favourite meals. Because finding African restaurants, especially those that served plant-based meals, was really hard, I always ended up settling for other restaurants that had plant-based options. I would then go home and try to make some of the dishes I had tasted without having the original recipes. Instead, I would rely on the flavour profile of the dishes and substitute most of the ingredients with indigenous African ones and expect the same results. I had trained my taste buds to do more than enjoy food but also to taste ingredients individually.

When I decided to go plant-based in my early twenties, my love of food and passion for cooking grew. I wanted to cook food that tasted as good as, if not better than, what I was used to as a meat-eater. When using plant-based ingredients, I became passionate about developing recipes with perfect textures, aroma and taste that are similar to the ones I have loved since my childhood. What was awakened in me was more than a passion, but a burning desire to start a revolution of taking African plant-based food to the world.

The more I developed new recipes that represent different countries on the continent, the more I found joy in cooking again and I came to the realisation that cooking is an art. It's my kind of art – the kind I don't want to keep to myself. Food has become a way of expressing myself and my means to serve each one of you, my continent and the world.

EMBRACE MISTAKES, EMBRACE SUCCESS

As you dive into these recipes, remember that cooking is an evolving art. Mistakes often lead to the best discoveries, so embrace them. Who knows? You may end up creating your own recipes inspired by unexpected moments, just as I did.

The other day I was trying to make oat breakfast bars. I left them in the oven for too long and they were like rocks! I then realised I had just made gluten-free vegan oat rusks, which were amazing with tea. And once I was so broke that I didn't even have soya milk for my porridge, yet I really wanted oats. I decided that since milk is milk, I might as well use the can of coconut milk that I had, and I have never tasted a yummier bowl of oats. I haven't looked back!

My love of cooking came out of a realisation that when you try something new and different you are bound to make mistakes. Through mistakes you learn that there are so many ways of doing things, so don't be afraid to make mistakes as you tackle some of the recipes in this book. Who knows, you might come up with new recipes born from those mistakes, just like my recipe for rusks here.

NOTE:

- Store in an airtight container.

Rusks

MAKES 40

- 500 g (4 cups) gluten-free self-raising flour (e.g. oat or rice flour)
- 1 tsp salt
- 120 g (1½ cups) oats
- 250 g (1¼ cups) granulated sugar
- 75 g (½ cup) raisins
- 40 g (⅓ cup) cranberries
- 50 g (⅓ cup) sunflower seeds
- 50 g (⅓ cup) pumpkin seeds
- 20 g (¼ cup) shelled hemp seeds (also known as hemp hearts)
- 30 g (¼ cup) flax meal
- 80 ml (⅓ cup) water
- 250 ml (1 cup) soya milk
- 1 tbsp apple cider vinegar
- 110 g (½ cup) coconut oil, melted

1. Preheat the oven to 180 °C (350 °F).
2. In a large bowl, sift the flour. Add the salt, oats, sugar, raisins, cranberries and all the seeds to the bowl. Mix until well combined.
3. In a small bowl, combine the flax meal with the water. Mix well and set aside.
4. In a separate bowl, mix the milk and vinegar. Let it sit for a few minutes until it thickens to a buttermilk consistency.
5. Add the coconut oil and flax mixture to the vegan buttermilk. Whisk until well combined.
6. Pour the wet ingredients into the dry ingredients. Mix until a thick, dough-like batter forms. If the mixture seems too dry, add a splash more liquid (water, plant milk, etc.). It should be sticky but not overly wet.
7. Line a rectangular baking tin (preferably 23 cm x 33 cm/9 inches x 13 inches with a rim of 3–5 cm/1½–2 inches) with baking paper.
8. Transfer the sticky dough to the lined baking tin and spread it out evenly. Bake for 45 minutes or until golden brown. To prevent over-browning, cover the tin with foil after 20 minutes of baking.
9. Once baked, remove from the oven and allow to cool in the tin for a few minutes, then transfer to a large chopping board to cool completely.
10. Once cool, cut the "cake" into finger-sized pieces. (Be careful not to cut them too thick.)
11. Place the cut rusks on a large flat baking sheet, leaving some space between each piece. Dry them out in a low oven (60 °C/140 °F) for 8–9 hours or until completely dry. If the pieces are thicker, they may need a little extra drying time.
12. Once dried, your rusks are ready to be dunked into your favourite beverage.

FINDING INSPIRATION

One of the questions I'm frequently asked is: "Where did your love of cooking come from and when did it start?" The honest answer is that my love of cooking developed in stages. The actual starting point is when I was a little girl – about seven years old.

When my older brother Leonard was a teenager, he was a renowned cook in the neighbourhood. This was very unusual because we were living in a society that did not encourage male children to pursue cooking as a hobby. Nor did we have access to global male chefs from whom he could draw some inspiration. I genuinely don't know how he got the exposure that led to his interest in and passion for the culinary arts. All I remember is that he inspired me.

I was so impressed by his passion whenever he cooked. As I mentioned earlier, his omelette-making skills were second to none. I remember watching him make one once. I was mesmerised by everything he did, from the way he chopped the onions to how he flipped the omelette by tossing it in the air. I didn't know it at the time, but I can safely say that, slowly but surely, my love of the kitchen was being cultivated.

And in honour of my brother, who inspired my journey in the kitchen, I decided to "veganise" his omelette while giving it an African twist.

Umureti Wa Okara

MAKES 1

Vegan Omelette with Okra

- 130 g (1 cup) chickpea flour (if possible, use chana flour from Indian stores – it works better)
- 40 g (¼ cup) rice flour or plain (all-purpose) flour
- 1 tbsp nutritional yeast (optional)
- ¼ tsp black salt (kala namak) or regular salt
- 1 tsp baking powder
- 160 ml (⅔ cup) water (add gradually as needed)
- 1 small onion, finely diced
- 1 garlic clove, finely diced
- Handful of fresh coriander (cilantro), finely chopped
- 1 tbsp oil for frying (e.g. sunflower oil), plus extra as needed
- 50 g (¼ cup) okra, sliced into rings

1. In a mixing bowl, combine the chickpea flour, rice flour, yeast (if using), salt and baking powder. Stir until well mixed.
2. Gradually add 80 ml (⅓ cup) of the water, mixing until you have a smooth paste.
3. Slowly incorporate the remaining water (up to 160 ml/⅔ cup total), stirring until the batter is smooth and slightly runny, like crepe batter. Set aside.
4. Add the onion, garlic and coriander to the omelette batter and mix well.
5. Heat the oil in a non-stick pan over medium heat. Add the okra in a single layer and fry for about 2 minutes on one side, then flip and fry for an additional minute until tender.
6. Pour the omelette batter over the cooked okra using a measuring cup to control the amount and achieve a thin, crepe-like consistency.
7. Cover the pan with a lid to steam the omelette. Cook on low-medium heat for about 5 minutes.
8. After 5 minutes, carefully loosen the edges of the omelette with a spatula. Flip it over and cook for an additional 3–5 minutes without the lid until the centre is firm.
9. Slide the omelette onto a plate and serve with your favourite vegetables.

NOTE:

- Kala namak or black salt gives this dish an egg smell but if you don't have it, normal salt will do.

WHAT IS OKRA?

The origins of okra can be traced back to Ethiopia, even though it has since spread to both North and West Africa. Okra is now a big part of West African cuisine and has since become popular across the continent. This beautiful hairy seed pod from the melon family, which is also known as ladies' fingers, happens to be an excellent source of vitamins C and K_1.

FROM AFRICA TO THE WORLD

I could have written a cookbook on anything, but it was important for me to write about African cuisine.

The other day I missed my friend Bongani's phone call and when I finally got back to her, she told me that she just wanted to rant about the price of fonio (an ancient West African grain) in South Africa. What she didn't know was that I had been having the same thought. It was good speaking to someone who felt the same way I did, and it wasn't just the issue of price for me, but also the inaccessibility. How can it be easier to find quinoa in Africa than it is to find fonio, which grows here? Why are African ingredients extremely hard to source? Why is African food looked down on?

Africa is one of the largest continents in the world and has diverse cultures and people, and African food is as good and diverse as its people. From east to west, north to south, African food has been proven to be delicious by those who have taken a chance on it. Yet regardless of how amazing, versatile and even healthy most African food is, African cuisine has not yet made any strides in the culinary world.

Since colonisation, Africans have often been marginalised and faced numerous prejudices. As a result, their cultural expressions have been devalued, including their cuisine, which in turn has discouraged them from promoting their culinary traditions. This has robbed the world of Africa's colourful and healthy way of living. African food has also been diluted by colonialism and people have forgotten what African food is. Many assume that African food is meat and mealie pap, which is actually far from the original diet of African people.

Our forefathers lived off the land. Their diet consisted mainly of plant-based foods such as ground roots, fruits and greens. Meat was either not on the menu or was eaten during cultural ceremonies and on other special occasions. Animals were seen as a symbol of wealth and wise people don't eat their wealth overnight. Having the knowledge, access and freedom to grow wholesome foods allowed our forefathers to not only live longer but also to thrive while doing so.

We are now living in a world in which young Africans want to decolonise everything introduced to them by the Western world and form their own world view based on their forefathers' principles. One of the changes I personally want to contribute to is shifting the view on African cuisine by bringing back traditional cooking and reviving ancestral food practices across the continent. I want the world to understand what Africans eat, where it came from and what our land produces. I also want to share the understanding of what was borrowed from non-African cuisines through colonisation and how Africans have managed to incorporate these items into their way of life. I know I'm not the only one on this journey, but I also know that the world is waiting for an African contribution in the culinary space. Furthermore, the world at large is finally prepared to learn, and I believe it starts here – with us sharing.

THE PLANT-BASED AFRICAN PANTRY

Ingredients are out there, so look out for them! Visit some of the ethnic stores around you that you've never stepped foot in, and you may well find that they have what you need. In addition, if there is a new or "strange" methodology for preparing some dishes, try it out and, while you're at it, add your own touch. That is how one becomes a master of this art.

If you can't find some of the original ingredients, don't worry. This list also includes alternatives that you can use instead, so you can still enjoy authentic African flavours with what's available to you. Finally, nowadays, we can order a much wider variety of unfamiliar foods online.

GRAINS + STARCHES

Bulgur wheat

North Africa: Morocco, Tunisia
Substitute: Couscous or cracked wheat

Cassava flour

Rwanda, Uganda, DRC, Tanzania, Ghana, Côte d'Ivoire, Nigeria, Liberia, Mozambique, Angola, Zambia, Malawi
Substitute: Potatoes or tapioca starch

Enset (false banana)

Ethiopia
Substitute: Taro root or potatoes

Fonio

Mali, Guinea, Senegal, Burkina Faso
Substitute: Quinoa or couscous

Fonio flour

Guinea, Senegal, Mali
Substitute: Quinoa flour or millet flour

Maize flour

Kenya, Uganda, Tanzania, Ghana, Nigeria, Sierra Leone, South Africa, Zimbabwe, Zambia, Malawi, Botswana
Substitute: Polenta or cornmeal

Matoke (green bananas)

Uganda, Rwanda
Substitute: Plantains or sweet potatoes

Millet

Niger, Mali, Senegal, Mauritania, Malawi, Zambia, Namibia, Zimbabwe, Angola, Botswana
Substitute: Quinoa or bulgur wheat

Pearl millet

Substitute: Couscous or quinoa

Plantains

Ghana, Côte d'Ivoire, Nigeria, Togo
Substitute: Green bananas or sweet potatoes

Pumpkin and squash

Zimbabwe, Zambia, South Africa, Malawi
Substitute: Butternut squash or acorn squash

Sorghum

Kenya, Uganda, Tanzania, Benin, Burkina Faso, Niger, Nigeria, Sudan, Lesotho, Botswana, Namibia, South Africa
Substitute: Brown rice or barley

Teff

Ethiopia
Substitute: Quinoa or millet

LEGUMES + PULSES

Bambara groundnuts

Uganda, Kenya, Tanzania, Ghana, Nigeria, Côte d'Ivoire, Zimbabwe, Botswana, Malawi, Zambia
Substitute: Chickpeas or pinto beans

Black-eyed beans (cowpeas)

Kenya, Uganda, Tanzania, Ghana, Nigeria, Senegal, Angola, Mozambique, Zambia, Malawi
Substitute: Black beans or kidney beans

Lentils

Ethiopia, Uganda, North Africa
Substitute: Split peas or chickpeas

Lupin beans

Morocco, Algeria
Substitute: Broad beans (fava beans) or chickpeas

Mung beans

Kenya, Uganda
Substitute: Lentils or split peas

Peanuts (groundnuts)

Sudan, Uganda, Tanzania, DRC, Nigeria, Ghana, Mali, Senegal, Malawi, Zambia, Zimbabwe, Mozambique

Tiger nuts

Nigeria, Ghana, DRC
Substitute: Almonds or hazelnuts

VEGETABLES

Amaranth greens

Kenya, Uganda, Rwanda, Togo, Benin, Nigeria, South Africa, Zimbabwe, Zambia
Substitute: Spinach or Swiss chard

Baobab leaves

Senegal, Mali, Kenya
Substitute: Spinach or moringa leaves

Butternut squash

South Africa, Zimbabwe, Malawi
Substitute: Pumpkin or acorn squash

Cassava leaves

Sierra Leone, Liberia, Rwanda, DRC, Angola, Mozambique, Zambia
Substitute: Spinach or collard greens

Cowpea leaves

Zambia, Zimbabwe, Namibia
Substitute: Kale or collard greens

Garden eggs (African eggplant)

DRC, Rwanda, Nigeria, Ghana
Substitute: Eggplant (aubergine) or courgette (zucchini)

Okra

Sudan, Somalia, Nigeria, Ghana, Sierra Leone, North Africa
Substitute: Courgette (zucchini) or green beans

Pumpkin leaves

Uganda, Rwanda, Kenya, Nigeria, Sierra Leone
Substitute: Kale or collard greens

Roselle leaves (sour leaves)

Mali, Senegal
Substitute: Sorrel or hibiscus leaves

Sukuma wiki (collard greens)

Kenya, Uganda, Tanzania
Substitute: Kale or Swiss chard

TUBERS, ROOTS + RHIZOMES

Cassava (tapioca)

Nigeria, Ghana, DRC, Rwanda, Uganda
Substitute: Sweet potatoes or yams

Cocoyams

Nigeria, Ghana
Substitute: Sweet potatoes or yams

Ginger roots

Nigeria, Ghana, Uganda, South Africa

Sweet potatoes

Rwanda, Uganda, Tanzania, Liberia, Ghana, Nigeria, Zimbabwe, Zambia, Malawi

Yams

Nigeria, Côte d'Ivoire, Ghana, Togo
Substitute: Sweet potatoes or russet potatoes

HERBS + SPICES

African basil (scent leaf)

Nigeria, Ghana
Substitute: Basil or Thai basil

Berbere

Ethiopia
Substitute: A mix of cayenne pepper, paprika, cinnamon, cumin and ginger

Panado
BENNY

Fenugreek
Ethiopia
Substitute: Maple syrup or mustard seeds

Ginger
Malawi, Mozambique, South Africa

Peri-peri
Mozambique, Angola
Substitute: Cayenne pepper or chilli flakes

Pilau masala
Kenya, Tanzania
Substitute: Garam masala or a mix of cinnamon, cardamom, cumin and cloves

Thyme (local)
Kenya, Nigeria, Ghana

Tsire (spice blend)
Nigeria, Ghana
Substitute: Miso paste or chickpea paste

Uziza leaves
West Africa: Nigeria
Substitute: Peppery rocket (arugula) or black pepper

Harissa
Somalia, Sudan, North Africa
Substitute: Sriracha or chilli paste

Shiro
Ethiopia
Substitute: Chickpea flour-based stews

Suya spice
Kenya, Tanzania, Nigeria
Substitute: A mix of cayenne pepper, garlic, paprika and peanuts

FERMENTED + PRESERVED STAPLES

Dawadawa (fermented locust beans)
Sudan, Nigeria, Ghana, Mali
Substitute: Miso paste or soya sauce

Egusi (melon seeds)
Nigeria, Ghana
Substitute: Pumpkin seeds or sunflower seeds

Gbegiri (bean paste)
West Africa: Nigeria
Substitute: Refried beans or mashed lentils

Injera
Ethiopia
Substitute: Sourdough bread or crepes

Kimere/Mabele/Fermented sorghum
Uganda, Sudan, South Africa, Botswana, Zimbabwe
Substitute: Sourdough or fermented porridge

CONDIMENTS & SAUCES

Akabanga chilli oil
Rwanda

FRUIT + NUTS

African breadfruit (ukwa)
Nigeria
Substitute: Jackfruit or breadfruit

African chewing gum (African star apple)
Malawi, Zimbabwe

Baobab fruit
Senegal, Kenya, Zimbabwe, South Africa
Substitute: Vitamin C-rich fruits such as acerola or camu camu

Bitter kola
Nigeria, Ghana
Substitute: Raw cacao nibs

Dates
Sudan, Somalia, North Africa
Substitute: Dried prunes

Kola nuts
Nigeria, Ghana
Substitute: Coffee or black tea

FATS + OILS

African red palm oil
Nigeria, Ghana
Substitute: Coconut oil

Argan oil
Morocco
Substitute: Olive oil

Shea butter
Nigeria, Ghana, Burkina Faso
Substitute: Coconut oil or ghee (if used in cooking)

REPRESENTING YOUR FOOD WELL

There are many misconceptions attached to African food, which are highlighted in the following comments I received while conducting a survey on how people felt about African cuisine. Some people said: "The only African food I was introduced to was too starchy, too heavy and too meaty." Others said: "African food doesn't look appetising and lacks sophistication."

These misconceptions are due to a lack of proper representation of what African cuisine really has to offer. Traditional African foods are a huge part of cultural preservation, and as African cuisine becomes popular and available to the global market, it will give the world a chance to learn about Africa's diverse cultures.

Moreover, it will give all Africans across the world a strong sense of pride in their heritage and the courage to express their African identity through their food, thereby making them true African ambassadors. I believe that Africans have a responsibility to challenge the bias against African food. This will not only help them find the healing they desperately need but also bring them closer to the land that has been feeding them.

It takes a lot of emotional effort to prepare, create, discover, explore, invent and taste when it comes to food. Thus, food sits on a raised emotional throne. As we share our food with others as a continent, we are sending out an invitation to them to come closer; to get to know us at an emotional level. As we open our cuisine to them, we open our hearts, share our pride and expose who we truly are.

WHAT IS AMARANTH?

Amaranth is a very popular traditional leafy vegetable around Africa. Its nutritional value and the ease with which it can be cultivated have made it popular in African countries, although its origin is Mexico. Amaranth leaves are a good source of iron and beta-carotene. The plant usually grows without any extra help and that's why it's easily found in the wild. It's drought tolerant, which means it's good for the environment too. Amaranth is the type of plant that can easily be grown in a garden, as it requires very little maintenance.

SOUTH AFRICA

ONE

WHEN THE RAINBOW NATION EXTENDS INTO FOOD

I spent most of my life in South Africa. My family moved from Kenya to South Africa when I was 13 years old. I was fascinated by how diverse everything was – I had never seen so many people of different races and cultures in one place as I did in South Africa. Soon I came to learn that the diversity extended to South African cuisine. When we arrived in South Africa we stayed with Gogo Moyo, who adopted our entire family and moved us into her home. We were complete strangers from across the continent, and she took us in, fed us and made sure we were acquainted with life in South Africa. Even though we were not biologically related to her, she insisted we call her "Gogo" (Grandma). When I talk about African hospitality, my entry into South Africa is filled with practical examples, such as the recipes on the following pages.

A PLATE OR SPREAD OF SEVEN COLOURS LUNCH

Although we met a lot of people who made our transition into South Africa easy and stress-free, the food transition was not that straightforward.

I grew up in a Seventh Day Adventist home. We spent the whole day at church on Saturdays and that meant church potluck. We ate together as a congregation as we waited for the afternoon church programme to start, and I remember tasting beetroot for the first time during one of the potlucks. I also recall tasting the most delicious butternut puree with cinnamon and I was amazed at how sugar was incorporated into savoury dishes. I now have a better understanding, but at the time this was such a new concept for someone who was used to sugar only being used in sweet dishes such as desserts.

In many South African homes, meals like this are called "seven colours" because of their variety. The name refers to the colourful mix of dishes on the plate, often including staples like pumpkin, beetroot, cabbage, salads and spiced vegetables. Though it was once simply called "several colours", the tradition has come to be known as "seven colours".

This spread comes together so nicely, and it was always made perfect by a large spoon of Gogo Moyo's homemade achar (a pickle using spices and oil), which she made using mangoes that grew in her backyard.

Chakalaka

SERVES 4 AS A SIDE DISH

Vegetable Relish

- 60 ml (¼ cup) grapeseed or other vegetable oil
- 1 medium onion, diced
- 1 tsp curry powder
- 2 tsp garlic, minced
- ½ tsp dried thyme
- ½ tsp smoked paprika
- ½ tsp ginger, minced
- 1 tsp ground cumin
- 1 medium green bell pepper, diced
- 1 medium red bell pepper, diced
- 1 large carrot, grated
- 2 tomatoes, finely diced
- 1–2 jalapeños, diced (seeds removed for less heat)
- 1 tbsp vegetable stock powder (optional)
- 1 tbsp apricot jam
- 1 tsp apple cider vinegar
- 1 can (425 g/15 oz) baked beans

1. In a large saucepan, heat the oil over medium heat. Add the onion and sauté for 1–2 minutes until it begins to soften.
2. Stir in the curry powder, garlic, thyme, paprika, ginger and cumin. Cook for about 1 minute, stirring continuously, to release the flavours.
3. Add the peppers, carrot, tomatoes and jalapeños. Mix well. Allow the mixture to simmer for about 5 minutes, stirring occasionally to prevent sticking or burning. If using, stir in the stock powder.
4. Stir in the apricot jam, vinegar and baked beans. Mix until well combined.
5. Allow the chakalaka to heat through for another 5–10 minutes, stirring occasionally.
6. Serve as a side dish. Chakalaka tastes good served warm or cold.

NOTES:

- Adjust the heat by varying the number of jalapeños or omitting them entirely.
- Feel free to add other vegetables based on your preference.

isiBokozi

SERVES 4 AS A SIDE DISH

Mashed Butternut Squash

- 1 butternut squash (approximately 1.8–2.3 kg/4–5 lb)
- Splash of oil for roasting (e.g. grapeseed or other vegetable oil)
- 1 tbsp brown sugar (optional)
- Pinch of salt, plus extra to taste
- 80 g (3 oz) vegan butter, melted
- Handful of fresh coriander (cilantro) leaves, chopped
- ¼ tsp ground cinnamon

1. Preheat the oven to 180 °C (350 °F).
2. Using a vegetable peeler, remove the skin from the butternut. Cut it lengthwise down the middle and remove the seeds, then wash the butternut. Cut it into bite-sized cubes.
3. Place the butternut in a roasting pan. Drizzle with a splash of oil and add the brown sugar (if using) and a pinch of salt. Mix well to ensure the butternut is evenly coated.
4. Roast for about 30 minutes or until the butternut is very tender.
5. Transfer the roasted butternut to a large mixing bowl. Using a potato masher or an electric hand mixer (a hand mixer will give a creamier texture) on low speed, mash the butternut until smooth. Stir in the butter and coriander.
6. Season with additional salt and the cinnamon, adjusting to your taste.
7. Serve warm.

Uspinashi Oqumbiwe

SERVES 4 AS A SIDE DISH

Creamed Spinach

- 1 kg (2.2 lb) fresh spinach leaves
- 125 ml (½ cup) water
- 1 tbsp vegan butter
- 1 small white onion, chopped
- 3 garlic cloves, minced
- ½ tsp salt, plus extra to taste
- 1 tbsp plain (all-purpose) flour or cake flour
- 400 ml (1⅔ cups) coconut milk
- 100 g (1 cup) chopped button mushrooms

1. Wash the spinach thoroughly and remove and discard any thick stems. Shred the green leaves into smaller pieces.

2. Add the water to a large pot and bring it to a boil. Add the spinach and steam for 3–5 minutes, or until the leaves are wilted and bright green. Drain any excess water and set the spinach aside.

3. In a saucepan over medium heat, melt the butter. Add the onion and garlic, cooking for about 2 minutes until softened.

4. Stir in the salt and flour, whisking continuously until the mixture is well combined and slightly golden.

5. Gradually add the coconut milk while whisking to prevent lumps from forming.

6. Add the mushrooms and cook for an additional 5 minutes, allowing the flour to cook through and the sauce to thicken.

7. Stir the steamed spinach into the white sauce, mixing until well combined. Taste and adjust seasoning, adding more salt if necessary.

8. Serve warm as a side dish or over your favourite grains or over rice.

NOTE:

- Spinach leaves refer to the larger, mature spinach commonly found in South Africa, which looks similar to Swiss chard. So don't go for the baby spinach, but rather a rustic variety.

RISE AND SHINE: THE BREAD CHALLENGE

When my siblings and I found ourselves in a refugee camp in northern DRC we did not have electricity, so we cooked on a wood fire outside our tent. I was a beginner in the kitchen with limited resources and experience, and I always ran out of options of what to make. Whenever my sister had enough money, she would buy cake flour, but we didn't have an oven so we always needed to buy oil as well so that we could make mandazi (p. 110). When we arrived in South Africa and learnt that it was possible to cook bread in a pot of water, I wanted to kick myself. Why hadn't I thought of this when I was trying to make our meals more exciting in the refugee camp?

Ujeqe

MAKES 12 ROLLS

Steamed Bread

- 375 g (3 cups) bread flour, plus extra if needed
- Pinch of salt
- 100 g (½ cup) granulated sugar
- 1 tsp instant yeast
- 500 ml (2 cups) warm water (about 40 °C/105 °F)

1. In a large mixing bowl, combine the flour, salt, sugar and yeast. (Mix the salt into the flour first before adding the sugar and yeast. This prevents direct contact between the salt and yeast, which can inhibit yeast activity.)
2. Make a well in the centre of the dry ingredients and pour in the warm water. Mix until a firm dough forms that doesn't stick to your hands. If the dough is too sticky, add a little more flour as needed.
3. Cover the bowl with a clean kitchen towel or clingfilm and let the dough rise in a warm place for about 1 hour or until it has doubled in size.
4. Once risen, gently knock the dough down to release the air. Divide it into 12 equal pieces and shape each piece into a ball. Place each ball of dough into individual small cups or ramekins.
5. Fill a large pot with water, ensuring the water level is below the top of the cups. If your pot isn't large enough to fit all 12 cups, steam in batches. Bring the water to a boil. Once boiling, carefully place the cups with the dough into the pot. Cover the pot with a lid.
6. Steam for about 20–25 minutes or until the bread is cooked through. (To check, insert a toothpick into the centre of the bread; it should come out clean.)
7. Serve warm with your favourite dishes or as part of a traditional seven colours lunch (p. 36).

NOTES:

- Using bread flour instead of cake flour enhances the bread's texture because it enables the gluten network to develop more effectively.
- This steamed bread pairs well with a variety of dishes, from savoury stews to sweet spreads.

A TASTE OF HOME

As much as I enjoyed the seven colours lunch (p. 36) and malva pudding (p. 46) during my time in Mbombela, our first home in South Africa, my heart still longed for some of the flavours and vegetables we used to eat back home in Rwanda.

One day my siblings and I discovered a bush full of amaranth leaves. To our surprise, it seemed as though no one was harvesting or eating them. The following day the whole household decided that we would go and harvest some of the leaves, which we would add to ground peanuts for a taste of home. As people passed by, they seemed confused that we were harvesting things they didn't consider to be food. Those who asked what we planned to do with the leaves were shocked when we told them that we were going to have them for supper.

It's been about 20 years since that incident and now that I have moved from Mbombela to Cape Town, I find myself having to go to a health store to buy amaranth seeds and leaves – something that was considered inedible by a whole community in Mbombela.

That's when I realised that the problem with Africa is not food security, it's food knowledge. It's sad having to go hungry when you are surrounded by food. This is one of the experiences that led me to my mission of helping people to understand the food that surrounds them and to learn to preserve what is harvested.

Imifino ye-Amaranth

SERVES 4

Cooked Amaranth Leaves

- 1 kg (2.2 lb) amaranth leaves
- 1 litre (4 cups) water
- 2 pinches of salt, plus extra to taste
- 1 tbsp grapeseed or other vegetable oil
- 1 large white onion, chopped
- 1 tsp minced ginger
- 4 garlic cloves, minced
- 3 medium tomatoes, chopped
- 1 can (400 ml /13.5 fl. oz.) coconut cream or any other non-dairy cream
- Pepper to taste

1. Wash the amaranth leaves thoroughly and chop them into large chunks. In a large pot, bring the water and a pinch of salt to a boil over high heat.
2. Add the amaranth leaves and boil for about 8–10 minutes or until tender. Once cooked, drain the leaves and set aside in a bowl inside another bowl containing ice water.
3. In a pan over medium heat, add the oil. Once the oil is hot, add the onion and sauté until golden brown (about 5–7 minutes). Add the ginger and garlic, stirring for about 1 minute until fragrant.
4. Stir in the tomatoes and season with a pinch of salt. Cook until the tomatoes are soft and mushy (about 5 minutes).
5. Pour in the coconut cream, stir well and continue cooking for 5 minutes.
6. Drain the amaranth leaves well and add them to the tomato mixture, stirring to combine.
7. Continue cooking the stew on medium heat for an additional 3 minutes, allowing the flavours to meld. Season with salt and pepper to taste.
8. Serve warm with rice or any other staple food of your choice.

NOTES:

- This stew pairs well with rice, fufu (a West African dish of boiled and pounded root vegetables) or any other African food carrier (a staple side that is commonly served alongside stews and sauces to complement the meal).
- Feel free to add other vegetables or proteins such as cooked chickpeas to the stew for added nutrition.

SOWING THE SEEDS OF WISDOM

I grew up on amaranth. We had a garden full of it and ate the leaves every other day in Rwanda. Despite having eaten this healthy vegetable for years, it never occurred to my family and me that amaranth seeds were also edible. When we prepared amaranth, we used to remove the seeds and discard them, until one day I was browsing through the aisles of a health store and saw that they were selling amaranth seeds. I was so shocked! I bought a packet to take home so I could tell everyone who cared to listen that amaranth seeds were being sold in stores.

I did more research to understand the benefits of the seeds and started experimenting with them in the kitchen. It saddened me that we had been wasting the seeds up until then. I was happy that I could finally use these beautiful seeds not only to make popcorn but also to add them to my diet as a replacement for rice. This is how the following recipe was born.

Amaranth Risotto

SERVES 4

- 4 tbsp coconut oil
- 1 yellow onion, finely chopped
- 2–3 garlic cloves, finely chopped
- 700 g (1½ lb) amaranth seeds
- 1 litre (4 cups) vegetable broth
- ¼ cup nutritional yeast
- Sea salt to taste
- 500 g (1 lb 2 oz) mushrooms, finely chopped
- 1 tbsp soya sauce
- 10 g (⅓ oz) parsley, chopped

1. In a large saucepan over medium heat, add 2 tbsp coconut oil.
2. When the oil is melted, add the onion. Cook, stirring often, until softened (about 5 minutes), then add the garlic and stir for 1 minute.
3. Add the amaranth seeds and briefly toast them. Don't allow them to change colour – 2–3 minutes should be enough.
4. Pour in the broth, starting with 250 ml (1 cup) and adding more slowly as it thickens. Cook, stirring often, until the risotto is soft. Twenty minutes was enough for me on low-medium heat.
5. Add the yeast and stir to combine. Season with salt as needed.
6. While the risotto is cooking, in a separate pan over medium heat add the rest of the coconut oil. Once the oil has heated add the mushrooms and salt to taste.
7. Keep the pan on medium heat. Cook the mushrooms until well browned but not burnt and until the liquid has completely evaporated.
8. Reduce heat to low and pour in the soya sauce. Stir and cook for another 2–3 minutes.
9. Add half the mushrooms to the cooked risotto and combine well. Remove the risotto from the heat and transfer to a serving dish.
10. Top with the remaining mushrooms, sprinkle with parsley and serve. Cooked cherry tomatoes also work well as a topping.

LEARNING TO CHANGE THE NARRATIVE

Writing about African food is very difficult. Many Africans tend to look at food with a colonial eye and not from the perspective of their ancestral heritage. This has become the lens we use to measure food quality, instead of considering what is good for our bodies and the food's nutritional value.

When I was a little girl there were guava trees in our neighbourhood, with utterly delicious pink fruit. One day, one of the children we played with arrived with a different type of guava. They were big and white, and we were sceptical about them. Our friend then told us that these guavas were imported from Europe, and we immediately abandoned the guavas from our neighbourhood and started begging our friend for a piece of his fruit – without even tasting it. Looking back, this moment illustrates something deeper: how quickly we can devalue what is ours when we believe something foreign is better. This mindset, rooted in colonial influence, continues today – many people see African indigenous or traditional food as inferior to imported or Western food, even when local ingredients are nutritious and well suited to our lifestyles and everyday needs.

When we hear of French cuisine, we may think of sophistication and even romance. On the other hand, when we think of African indigenous food, we may think of poverty and dirt instead of health and desirability. As I write this book, I'm still in the process of transforming my mind. In choosing sorghum over maize, and fonio over pasta, I am learning to choose food best suited to my body's needs as I continue to look into what my ancestors thrived on instead of what the world has told me to eat. As I continue to figure out more about my forefathers' food narratives, I would like to transform the foods I eat by using ingredients that they ate, such as using tiger nut milk instead of cow's milk to make my desserts. This is how I developed these signature South African desserts.

Vegan Malva Pudding

SERVES 6 (MEDIUM PORTIONS)

For the sauce

- 250 ml (1 cup) non-dairy cream (e.g. Orley Whip or any plant-based cream)
- 125 g (4½ oz) coconut oil
- Pinch of salt
- 100 g (½ cup) granulated sugar
- 4 tbsp apricot jam

For the pudding

- 60 g (2¼ oz) coconut oil
- 150 g (¾ cup) granulated sugar
- 4 tbsp apricot jam
- 2 tbsp golden or brown flax meal (ground flaxseeds)
- 400 g (scant 3 cups) cake flour
- 1½ tsp baking powder
- 1 tsp bicarbonate of soda (baking soda)
- Pinch of salt
- 200 ml (scant 1 cup) soya milk (or any other plant-based milk)
- 4 tbsp vinegar (e.g. apple cider vinegar or rice vinegar)

1. To make the sauce, in a small saucepan combine the cream, coconut oil, salt, sugar and apricot jam.
2. Heat over low to medium heat, stirring continuously for about 2 minutes until the ingredients are well combined. Set aside.
3. Preheat the oven to 180 °C (350 °F).
4. To make the pudding, use an electric whisk (or a hand whisk) to cream the coconut oil and sugar together in a mixing bowl until light and fluffy.
5. Add the apricot jam and flax meal to the mixture, whisking well until fully incorporated.
6. Sift the flour, baking powder, bicarbonate of soda and salt together. Gradually add this to the coconut mixture, alternating with the milk. Mix until just combined.
7. Once the batter is smooth, add the vinegar and mix until light and fluffy.
8. Pour the batter into an oven-safe deep dish and bake for 20 minutes.
9. After 20 minutes, remove the pudding from the oven. Carefully pierce the surface several times with a skewer or fork to allow the sauce to absorb better.
10. Pour most of the sauce over the pudding and return it to the oven. Bake for an additional 15 minutes or until completely cooked through.
11. Once cooked, pour the remaining sauce over the pudding and let it sit in the switched-off oven for 5 minutes to soak in.
12. Serve warm, preferably with vegan ice cream, vegan custard or whipped non-dairy cream and apricot halves.

Vegan Milk Tart

SERVES 6–8 (SMALL TO MEDIUM PORTIONS)

For the crust

- 125 g (1 cup) cake flour
- 50 g (¼ cup) granulated sugar
- 1 tsp ground cinnamon
- 35 g (1¼ oz) vegan butter or margarine, cold

For the filling

- 250 ml (1 cup) tiger nut milk (or any non-dairy milk), plus extra to make a slurry
- 250 ml (1 cup) coconut cream
- 60 g (⅓ cup) granulated sugar
- 1 tsp vanilla extract
- ½ tsp ground cinnamon, plus extra for sprinkling
- 50 g (¼ cup) cornflour (cornstarch)

1. Preheat the oven to 180 °C (350 °F).
2. To make the crust, combine the flour, sugar and cinnamon in a large bowl. Cut in the butter until the mixture resembles soft playdough.
3. On a floured surface, roll out the dough to fit a pie dish.
4. Carefully transfer the rolled dough to the pie dish and press it into the bottom and up the sides. Prick the bottom with a fork to prevent bubbling.
5. Bake for about 20 minutes or until slightly golden. Remove from the oven and let it cool.
6. To prepare the filling, combine the milk, coconut cream, sugar, vanilla extract and cinnamon in a small saucepan. Bring to a gentle boil over medium heat, stirring frequently.
7. In a separate bowl, mix the cornflour with a small amount of cold milk to create a slurry. Gradually add this slurry to the boiling milk mixture, stirring continuously, until it thickens. Remove from heat.
8. Pour the thickened filling into the cooled pie crust and sprinkle with additional ground cinnamon.
9. Place the tart in the fridge for at least 1 hour to set before serving.
10. Serve chilled.

NOTES:

- Store any leftovers in the fridge for up to 3 days.
- Substitute almond, oat or soya milk for tiger nut milk if desired.

SLOWLY BECOMING THE PRIDE OF AFRICA

The world has become a global village. Everything has become so globalised that we sometimes forget our own way of living. Technology has made the world so small and has made other lifestyles easily accessible, but in the process, we have forgotten that our gut health does not change with technology. There is nothing wrong with progression – the problem is when people forget that the traditional foods of their ancestors were naturally suited to their nourishment.

Abena Offeh-Gyimah is an amazing woman who has become one of my favourite humans and a friend. She has decided to spend her life finding out how her African ancestors lived, and researching and protecting each seed they left behind. During one of our conversations, she mentioned that we often underestimate the power of a seed – the fact that there were people who died trying to preserve seeds so that our generation can find food that speaks to our DNA. The same seeds carry stories of our origins and teach us the ways of our ancestry. We have both concluded that lack of interest in our indigenous food is the easiest way to lose who we are as a people and what we can contribute to the world. Having said that, I really love how rooibos (red bush) tea has distinguished itself as one of Africa's best.

Whenever I watch a foodie on social media drinking a healthy tea, it often turns out to be rooibos. My dream is to one day see more of our African indigenous food getting as much recognition as rooibos is receiving.

Itiyi ye-Rooibos ene-Mint

SERVES 4

Mint Rooibos Iced Tea

1 litre (4 cups) water

4–5 rooibos tea bags (adjust based on desired strength)

A handful of fresh mint leaves, plus extra for garnish

Sweetener of your choice (e.g. sugar, agave syrup or maple syrup)

Juice of 1 lemon (about 60 ml/4 tbsp)

Lemon slices, for garnish

1. Boil the water in a kettle.
2. Pour the water into a large mixing jug. Add the tea bags and mint leaves to the hot water. Allow them to steep for 2–3 minutes, stirring gently with a spatula to help the extraction.
3. After steeping, remove the tea bags and mint leaves from the jug.
4. While the tea is still warm,add the lemon juice. Then add your preferred sweetener to taste. Stir well to combine.
5. Allow the tea to cool to room temperature, then place it in the fridge. Chill for a few hours or overnight until completely cold.
6. Serve the iced tea over ice cubes, garnished with additional fresh mint leaves and lemon slices.

NOTES:

- Experiment with adding more mint or other fruits and spices.
- Store any leftover iced tea in the fridge for up to 3 days.

Isobho ye-Rooibos

SERVES 4

Rooibos Sorbet

For the rooibos simple syrup	For the sorbet
250 ml (1 cup) water	1 sweet melon (e.g. cantaloupe or honeydew), peeled, seeded and cubed
175 g (scant 1 cup) granulated sugar	A handful of fresh mint leaves
2 tbsp loose leaf rooibos tea or 2 rooibos tea bags	Juice of ½ lemon (about 30 ml/ 2 tbsp)

MAKE THE ROOIBOS SIMPLE SYRUP

1. In a saucepan, combine the water, sugar and rooibos tea. Bring the mixture to a boil over medium heat.
2. Stir until the sugar has completely dissolved. Once dissolved, reduce the heat and let it simmer for an additional 5 minutes.
3. Remove from heat and discard the rooibos leaves (strain the mixture) or tea bags.
4. Allow the syrup to cool to room temperature.

PREPARE THE SORBET MIXTURE

1. In a blender, combine the cubed sweet melon, fresh mint leaves and lemon juice. Blend until smooth.
2. Once the rooibos syrup has cooled, combine it with the melon mixture in the blender. Blend again until fully combined.
3. Transfer the mixture to a container and refrigerate for at least 4 hours or until chilled.

CHURN THE SORBET

If using an ice cream maker

1. Following the manufacturer's instructions for your ice cream maker, pour the chilled mixture into the machine and churn for about 20 minutes. Transfer to a bowl and freeze until firm.

If not using an ice cream maker

1. Pour the chilled mixture into a shallow dish lined with parchment paper that can fit in your freezer. Freeze until completely frozen (about 4–6 hours).
2. Once frozen, break the sorbet into pieces and place them in a food processor. Blend until smooth. Serve immediately for a soft sorbet.

FOOD IN AFRICA

AFRICANS HAVE FAR MORE IN COMMON THAN NOT

As I have travelled around Africa, I have come to realise that my continent's people have far more in common than we might think. When I was a little girl and visited my grandparents in rural Rwanda with my family, we were always guaranteed that one of the dishes my grandmother would prepare for us was impungure. This was the Rwandan version of samp (dried corn kernels) and beans. My grandmother sometimes added unpeeled baby potatoes and seasoned it with salt. It was delicious, healthy and super simple. I was young at the time, but I still have vivid memories of it.

In every new chapter of my life, there is a new dish of samp and beans.

When I moved to Kenya, the samp and beans trend continued, but there it was called kitheri. When I arrived in Kenya as an 11-year-old who couldn't speak a word of English or Swahili, most of the time I felt out of place in the foreign environment. It was dishes such as kitheri that took me back to a familiar place and brought back familiar feelings.

Whenever I had change to spare, that's the dish I would buy from a woman who sold food outside our school gate. I loved how some of the Kenyan kitheri recipes incorporated fresh maize.

Years later I met my now best friend Khona in Cape Town. In my opinion, I think she makes the best umngqusho (samp and beans) I have ever tasted.

Maize is not an indigenous African grain, but I'm forever amazed at how adaptive Africans across the continent are; how we are able to take a foreign food and adapt it to our own way of living and make the best of it.

A HOMAGE TO HERITAGE

As I went down memory lane and learnt how African people have always been adventurous, I also attempted to develop my own samp and beans recipe inspired by my grandmother, the woman who sold food at my school gate and my friend Khona.

I hate to blow my own trumpet, but my samp and beans taste delicious! By combining my grandmother's simplicity and her love of anything potatoes with fresh sweetcorn and creamy avocado as a reminder of my primary school days in Kenya, as well as Khona's seasonings and spices, I ended up with an incredibly tasty dish.

Umngqusho

Samp and Beans

SERVES 6 AS A MAIN DISH

- 300 g (10½ oz) samp (dried corn kernels)
- 200 g (7 oz) sugar beans or any preferred beans
- Salt to taste
- 1–1.5 litres (4–7 cups) water

For the vegetables

- 400 g (14 oz) baby potatoes, halved or quartered
- 1 tbsp olive or grapeseed oil
- 1 medium onion, chopped
- 2 garlic cloves, minced
- 1 medium red bell pepper, chopped
- 1 medium yellow bell pepper, chopped
- 1 medium green bell pepper, chopped
- 140 g (5 oz) frozen sweetcorn

For the seasoning

- 1 tbsp vegetable stock powder
- 1 tsp soya sauce
- Garlic and herb seasoning to taste
- Salt and pepper to taste
- Fresh herbs, for garnish
- Avocado (optional, for serving)

1. Soak the samp and sugar beans in water overnight. The next day, drain and rinse the samp and beans.
2. In a large pot, add the soaked samp and beans, season with salt and add 1–1.5 litres (4–7 cups) water. Cover and bring to a boil.
3. Reduce heat and let it simmer for approximately 1½ hours or until the samp and beans are tender and most of the water has been absorbed. Halfway through cooking, add the baby potatoes to the pot.
4. In a separate saucepan, heat the oil over medium heat. Add the onion and sauté for about 2 minutes until softened.
5. Add the garlic and peppers. Sauté for an additional 2 minutes until the peppers are tender.
6. Stir in the sweetcorn and cook for another minute until heated through.
7. Add the stock powder, soya sauce and a splash of boiling water (about 120 ml/½ cup) to the vegetable mixture. Stir well.
8. Add garlic and herb seasoning to taste. Pour the vegetable mixture into the pot with the cooked samp and beans. Mix well and cook on low heat for another 10 minutes to combine the flavours. Taste and adjust seasoning with more salt and pepper as needed.
9. Plate the dish and garnish with fresh herbs and slices of avocado, if using.
10. Serve warm as a hearty meal or side dish.

NOTES:

- Using frozen sweetcorn is convenient and adds sweetness to the dish without the need for thawing beforehand.
- Feel free to substitute with any type of beans, such as black beans or kidney beans.
- Fresh coriander, parsley or spring onions (scallions) make a lovely garnish.
- This dish pairs well with a simple green salad.

WHAT IS ROOIBOS?

Rooibos is a South African indigenous tea. The leaves of the plant have been used for generations by the San and Khoi people as a remedy for different illnesses. Unlike black or green tea, this herbal tea is free from caffeine. It has zero calories and although it doesn't have a lot of nutritional value, it is rich in antioxidants. It also contains trace amounts of minerals such as iron, calcium, magnesium, potassium, zinc, manganese, fluoride and copper.

MOZAM BIQUE

TWO

THE MARVELLOUS RIVERS OF MOZAMBIQUE

I get seasick. It's so bad that at the sight of water, everything inside me starts moving. When I was in school, and all the other learners were excited about a school trip to Robben Island (where South African freedom fighters including Nelson Mandela were imprisoned), the thought of being in a boat terrified me so much that I ended up not going. Even to this day I haven't been to Robben Island.

There were, however, many other occasions when I had no choice but to find myself in the middle of water. My vivid memory of Mozambique is my family and I crossing a river in a boat. I was terrified! It was during a heavy flood, and apart from closing my eyes, the only thing that helped me get through to the other side was knowing that I'd soon be having lunch, since it was almost lunchtime, and there were a number of restaurants across the river.

The people of Mozambique have always depended on rivers, which have been their source of fresh water and play a big role in food growth and other agricultural purposes. The riverbanks have coconut trees that provide food that is used daily.

What makes Mozambique's rivers so special is that the country shares most of them with other African countries such as Zambia, Tanzania and Malawi. This creates opportunities for connection and cooperation to protect this natural beauty. It's wonderful how nature keeps finding a way of uniting us and bringing us together in our quest to protect it.

Just as I can't forget Mozambique's rivers, once you have visited Mozambique you will definitely remember the food! Since the country is on the coast, almost every dish has coconut in it. Mozambican dishes are not that different from what I grew up eating, but I always found the idea of additional coconut fascinating and simply delicious.

Xiguinha

SERVES 4–6

Cassava with Peanut Powder and Greens

250 g (9 oz) spinach leaves (or any greens of your choice, e.g. amaranth)

Pinch of salt

1 tbsp grapeseed or other vegetable oil

1 medium onion, chopped

3 garlic cloves, minced

500 g (1 lb 2 oz) cassava tuber, cut into cubes

1 litre (4 cups) coconut milk

240 g (2 cups) ground peanuts

1 tsp seasoning cube powder or salt to taste (optional)

1. Thoroughly wash the spinach leaves to remove any dirt.
2. In a large pot, add the spinach leaves with a pinch of salt and enough water to cover them. Bring to a boil.
3. Once boiled (about 3–5 minutes), remove the spinach leaves and set them aside in an ice water bath, but keep the cooking water for later.
4. In a separate large pot, heat the oil over medium heat. Add the onion and sauté for about 2 minutes until translucent.
5. Stir in the garlic and cook for an additional minute until fragrant.
6. Add the cassava to the pot along with the reserved water from boiling the spinach leaves. Bring to a boil.
7. Reduce heat and simmer for about 10–15 minutes or until the cassava is tender when pierced with a fork. If there is excess water, drain it carefully.
8. Divide the cassava, leaving one half in the pot and setting the other aside. Spread out the cassava in the pot, pour over the coconut milk and top with the boiled greens.
9. Sprinkle half the peanuts on top of the greens.
10. Add the reserved cassava and layer it on top of the peanut mixture.
11. Top with the remaining peanuts and the rest of the cassava.
12. Place the pot over low heat and cover. Allow to simmer for about 20 minutes, stirring occasionally to prevent sticking. Cook for an additional 10 minutes to combine the flavours.
13. Adjust seasoning with seasoning cube powder or salt, if desired.
14. Serve warm as a hearty main dish or side dish.

NOTES:

- You can use any leafy greens such as kale, collard greens or Swiss chard.
- For a nuttier flavour, lightly toast the ground peanuts (they should have a powdery consistency like flour) before adding them to the dish. (With the pan on medium heat, roast the ground peanut flour, stirring frequently to prevent burning.)
- This dish pairs well with rice or can be enjoyed on its own.

CLASSIC CASSAVA GETS A COCONUT TWIST

Looking back at the traditional methods of preparing cassava leaves, it's clear you'd get quite a workout in the process. Even though this dish is so tasty, I doubt it would have made its way onto my menu even once a month. But now I make this dish at least once a week, as technology has made it easy to prepare it.

Traditionally, cassava leaves would be harvested from cassava trees, then pounded using a huge wooden pestle and mortar until the leaves became smooth. This took time and required muscles. Thanks to the advancement in technology, most of the work is done for us now. Though some older women would argue that the dish made using a pestle and mortar tastes much better than the ones that are blended, packaged and frozen, I call that resistance to change. For those of us who live in areas where there are no cassava trees, we buy the leaves already pounded and frozen, and we enjoy them just as much.

I love the delicious twist that Mozambique gives the dish by adding fresh coconut milk. When my sister Ngema, who lived in Mozambique for many years, introduced me to this idea, I was sold before I had even tasted it.

NOTES:

- Matapa can be served with rice, fufu or your choice of bread.
- Store leftovers in an airtight container in the fridge for up to 3 days.

Matapa

SERVES 6

Cassava Leaves

- 3 dried mushrooms (e.g. shiitake or porcini)
- ½ sheet nori (seaweed)
- 1 tbsp African red palm oil or vegetable oil
- 1 medium onion, chopped
- 3 garlic cloves, minced
- 1 tsp red curry paste
- 1 tbsp tomato paste
- 500 g (1 lb 2 oz) frozen cassava leaves
- 250 ml (1 cup) hot vegetable stock (or 250 ml/1 cup vegetable broth), plus extra if needed
- 120 g (1 cup) ground peanuts
- 70 g (½ cup) shredded soya chicken (or your favourite plant-based protein)
- 250 ml (1 cup) coconut milk
- 250 g (9 oz) button mushrooms, sliced
- 300 g (10½ oz) garden eggs or eggplant (aubergine), cut into halves
- 2 medium tomatoes, chopped
- 1 tbsp soya sauce
- Salt and pepper to taste

1. In a blender, grind the dried mushrooms and nori into a fine powder. This mixture serves as a substitute for crayfish, which is traditionally used in this dish to add umami flavour.
2. In a large saucepan, heat the oil over medium heat. Add the onion and garlic, and sauté for about 2 minutes until fragrant.
3. Stir in the red curry paste, tomato paste and dried mushroom-nori powder. Cook for another 1–2 minutes.
4. Stir in the frozen cassava leaves and enough hot vegetable stock to cover the mixture. Cover the pot and cook on medium heat for about 1 hour, stirring occasionally.
5. Add the peanuts and soya chicken to the pot. If the mixture appears too thick, add more water or stock as needed. Cover and cook for an additional 20 minutes.
6. Stir in the coconut milk, mushrooms, garden eggs, tomatoes and soya sauce. Cover the saucepan and continue cooking on low heat for about 20 more minutes, checking occasionally to prevent burning. Add salt and pepper to taste.
7. Serve warm with roasted peanuts and chilli peppers (to taste) as a hearty main meal or as a side dish.

POTATOES IN A PUDDING?

We can't talk about Mozambique without talking about cashew nuts. Whenever my sister Ngema visited us in Cape Town from Mozambique, my simple request to her would be: "Don't forget to bring me some cashew nuts." I love them so much that whenever she brought me some, I would hide them from my siblings.

Mozambique used to be the largest producer of cashew nuts before Côte d'Ivoire took over. These nuts used to be sold on the street like ordinary nuts, but now some of us need to save up to keep up with our cashew nut cravings.

My relationship with cashew nuts is a beautiful love affair. I add them to curries and vegan cheesecakes, and just snack on them whenever I can. When I was introduced to bolo Polana, I was hooked at the mention of cashew nuts, although I was sceptical about having potatoes in a dessert.

Bolo Polana is a Mozambican traditional dessert served on special occasions. This dense yet delicious dessert, named after a suburb in Mozambique, is packed with citrus flavours from zested oranges and lemon. It is rich with a creamy texture and nuttiness from the cashews, and mashed potatoes keep it smooth.

Vegan Bolo Polana

SERVES 6–8

Cashew Nut Cake

- 170 g (6 oz) vegan butter, plus extra for greasing
- 190 g (1²/₃ cups) plain (all-purpose) flour or cake flour, plus 30 g (4 tbsp) for dusting
- 400 g (2 cups) granulated sugar
- 4 tbsp ground flaxseeds (golden flaxseed works better in this recipe) mixed with 12 tbsp water (let sit for 5–10 minutes to thicken)
- 1 medium potato, peeled, boiled and mashed
- 150 g (5½ oz) ground cashew nuts
- Zest of 1 lemon
- Zest of 1 orange
- 125 ml (½ cup) coconut cream or any other plant-based cream
- 1 tbsp vanilla extract

1. Preheat the oven to 180 °C (350 °F). Prepare a springform pan by greasing it with butter and dusting it with flour.
2. In a large mixing bowl, cream the butter and sugar together until light and fluffy. Add the prepared flax egg mixture (the flaxseeds mixed with water) and mix well.
3. Stir in the potato, cashew nuts, lemon zest, orange zest, coconut cream and vanilla extract until well combined.
4. Gradually incorporate the flour into the mixture, stirring until smooth.
5. Pour the batter into the prepared cake pan. Bake for approximately 1 hour or until a toothpick inserted into the centre comes out clean.
6. Allow the cake to cool for about 10 minutes before removing it from the pan and slicing.

NOTES:

- Serve with a dusting of icing sugar (confectioners' sugar) or a scoop of non-dairy ice cream for extra indulgence.
- Store leftovers in an airtight container in the fridge for up to 5 days.

WHAT IS COCOYAM?

Cocoyam is a starchy, nutrient-rich root vegetable widely grown across many parts of Africa. Belonging to the same family as yam, it's prized for its versatility, lending itself to both savoury and sweet dishes, and is also high in fibre.

FOOD IN AFRICA

CASHING IN ON CASSAVA PLANTS

Where I come from, we call it isombe, in the DRC they call it pondu and in Mozambique it's known as matapa. This dish of cassava leaves is popular in Rwanda, but I have come to learn that it's just as popular in Mozambique and many other African countries.

All the way from the DRC, it made its way to Rwanda, where it has become a staple meal. The combination of fresh cassava leaves with ground peanuts results in a mouthwatering, delicious taste. Most people add different types of meat, but the vegan option is just as tasty, especially when you add oyster mushrooms or any other type of mushrooms to give it that meaty feel.

Don't forget to add some garden eggs, onion, peppers and garlic. These vegetables, which are cooked until tender, add a beautiful balance to the dish and make it hearty. I always add peanuts last; they are used as a thickener, and adding them too early may cause the food to burn.

ZAMBIA

THREE

WATER, ROOTS AND RHYTHM

Africans have had a fascination with water and rivers for centuries. Rivers are used for different ceremonial activities as an instrument of purification and to regenerate life. The abundance of water is a true form of wealth in some parts of Africa and it's through this abundance that we cultivate our livelihood. Zambia was named after the fourth-longest river in Africa, the Zambezi, and is connected to the source of life.

My desire is to visit this amazing place. However, I have been transported there through some Zambian dishes I have been privileged enough to taste. Food has taken me to places that I, for now, can only dream of visiting. Every time I taste something that brings rhythm to my taste buds, I stop for a second to reflect on the genius discovery of that particular food.

In 2017 I took part in a refugee food festival in Cape Town. Once a year, organisers of the festival create collaborations between refugee cooks and local restaurateurs in 15 cities around the world. It was through this festival that I was able to meet my new friend, chef David from the DRC. David and I share the same passion for food and the culinary arts. Long after the festival, we got in touch with each other and decided to start a few collaborations of our own. David was from a fine-dining background, and I was a simple cook who was fascinated by understanding great flavours. However, what we both have in common is the love of feeding people. With this in mind, we decided to start hosting dinners at my little apartment in Cape Town. And that's when I tasted chikanda for the first time.

THE REMARKABLE ORCHID SAUSAGE

During one of the pop-up dinners at my apartment, David's friend Veronica from Zambia was one of our guests. When she learnt that I was following a plant-based lifestyle, she mentioned a Zambian dish called chikanda and insisted that I needed to try it. At our next dinner, Veronica made chikanda for David and me to feed our guests. Let's just say that when I tasted it, I was blown away. When she mentioned that it was made from wild orchids, I was left speechless.

Chikanda is known to many as either Zambian sausage or African polony because of its taste and texture. It used to be served mainly during special ceremonies and when special guests such as in-laws visited. However, because of its popularity you will easily find it being sold to passers-by on the streets of Lusaka, the capital of Zambia.

I would have done great injustice to this book if I hadn't included this recipe, despite the difficulties I had trying to access the orchids on time. Chikanda is made from the ground tubers of certain wild orchids, which are either sold as a ready-made powder or can be ground at home. My dream world is a world in which African ingredients like these are easily accessible regardless of where we are in the world.

Chikanda

SERVES 6–8

African Polony

- About 1.5 litres (6 cups) plus 5 tbsp water
- 600 g (1 lb 5 oz) pounded groundnuts (peanuts) or peanut flour
- 1 tsp bicarbonate of soda (baking soda)
- 3 tsp salt
- 150 g (2/3 cup) ground chikanda powder
- Pinch of chilli powder (optional)

1. Preheat the oven to 180 °C (350 °F).
2. To a medium saucepan, add 1.5 litres of water. Stir in the groundnuts, bicarbonate of soda and salt, setting aside about 2 tbsp of the pounded groundnuts and a pinch of bicarbonate of soda for later.
3. Place the saucepan on medium heat and stir the mixture until it begins to boil.
4. Once boiling, gradually add the chikanda powder and the pinch of chilli powder (if using), stirring continuously.
5. As you stir, the mixture will thicken. Continue stirring until it becomes firm and no longer sticks to your stirring utensil.
6. In a separate bowl, mix the reserved 2 tbsp of pounded groundnuts with a pinch of bicarbonate of soda and 5 tbsp of water. Add this mixture to your pot slowly while continuing to stir the chikanda.
7. Pour the thickened chikanda mixture into an oven-proof container (preferably a metal pot) and spread it evenly with a wooden spoon.
8. Place the container in the preheated oven and bake for 20–30 minutes.
9. Check whether the chikanda is ready by inserting a toothpick or knife; it should come out clean.
10. Once done, allow it to cool slightly before slicing and serving.

NOTES:

- Adjust the chilli powder according to your heat preference.
- Ground chikanda powder can be sourced from speciality stores.

PEANUTS: A PRACTICAL POWERHOUSE

Something that shocked me to the core was finding out that peanuts are legumes, not nuts, and also that they are not an indigenous African food!

As much as peanuts are the backbone of cuisines around Africa, they were brought to the continent from South America by Portuguese colonisers, who also encountered them in Brazil on their way to Africa.

Africans have turned this humble nut, or should I say legume, into a delicacy. We eat them as snacks and use them as thickeners in our stews and soups. They also come in handy when making desserts and other sweet treats. We have truly found something special when it comes to peanuts. Allow me to highlight them here in all their glory.

Chibwabwa

SERVES 6

Peanut and Eggplant (Aubergine) Soup

- 1 tsp grapeseed or other vegetable oil
- 1 medium white onion, chopped
- 3 garlic cloves, minced
- 1 red bell pepper, diced
- 1 Scotch bonnet pepper, seeds removed and diced (optional)
- 2 medium eggplants (aubergines), peeled and diced
- 2 medium tomatoes, finely diced
- Salt to taste (e.g. pink Himalayan salt)
- 85 g (1/3 cup) natural peanut butter
- 1 litre (4 cups) vegetable broth, plus extra as needed
- 140 g (2 cups) kale leaves, destemmed and torn
- Handful of fresh coriander (cilantro), chopped, plus extra for garnish
- Roasted peanuts, for garnish

1. In a large saucepan, heat the oil over medium heat. Add the onion and garlic. Sauté for about 5 minutes or until the onion becomes translucent.

2. Stir in the bell pepper, Scotch bonnet pepper (if using), eggplants and tomatoes. Increase the heat to medium-high and simmer for an additional 5 minutes. Season the vegetables with salt to taste.

3. In a medium bowl, whisk together the peanut butter and 250 ml (1 cup) of vegetable broth until smooth and free of clumps. Pour this mixture into the saucepan along with the remaining 750 ml (3 cups) of vegetable broth. Cover the pan with a lid, reduce the heat to medium-low and let it simmer for 15–20 minutes.

4. Stir in the kale and cook until wilted. Taste and adjust seasoning with more salt if needed. Stir in the coriander, reserving some for garnish.

5. Ladle the soup into bowls and garnish with extra coriander and roasted peanuts. Serve with a food carrier such as rice, chapati, fufu or any preferred accompaniment.

GREENS AND GROUNDNUTS

While still on the subject of peanuts, I would like to introduce you to Zambian ifisashi (greens in peanut sauce). This is a concept that has been adopted by most countries in Africa, especially East and southern African countries, but it appears that it's only Zambia that has a name for it.

When I was growing up, it was almost second nature to add ground peanuts to any dish to thicken it. It was such a big part of how we cooked. Even now that there are thousands of thickeners on the market, peanuts are still my ultimate way to thicken my stews and soups. They not only add flavour but are also packed with nutrients. What's more, peanuts are right after soya beans when it comes to the recommended daily intake of plant protein.

When cooking for your family or friends, add some ground peanuts to your greens. My favourite greens to combine with groundnuts – and this also brings back so many childhood memories – are pumpkin leaves. And after I learnt that sweet potato leaves are also edible, these also became one of my favourites.

Zambian Ifisashi

SERVES 4–6

Assorted Greens with Ground Peanuts

- 1 bunch sweet potato leaves (or spinach leaves)
- 45 ml (3 tbsp) grapeseed or other vegetable oil
- 1 medium white onion, chopped
- 2 garlic cloves, minced
- 1 large tomato, chopped
- 200 g (7 oz) ground peanuts
- 1 tsp turmeric
- Salt to taste
- Water as needed

1. Wash the sweet potato leaves thoroughly. Remove the stalks.
2. In a medium saucepan, heat the oil over medium heat. Add the onion and garlic, and sauté until caramelised (about 5 minutes).
3. Stir in the tomato and cook until tender (about 3–4 minutes).
4. Add the sweet potato leaves to the saucepan. Cover the pot and cook for about 5 minutes until the leaves are wilted.
5. In a small bowl, mix the ground peanuts with a little water to create a smooth paste.
6. Add the peanut mixture to the pot with the sweet potato leaves. Stir well and season with turmeric and salt to taste.
7. Cook on low heat for an additional 15 minutes, stirring occasionally. If the mixture is too thick, add a little water to reach your desired consistency.
8. Enjoy your ifisashi with a food carrier of your choice such as rice, or thick maize porridges like sadza or nshima.

WHAT IS CHIKANDA?

Chikanda, commonly known as African polony, is made from terrestrial orchids that have been used for medicinal and culinary purposes for centuries. They grow naturally in the northern, northwestern and eastern regions of Zambia, but most chikanda tubers can be found in Tanzania.

TANZANIA

FOUR

WHEN IN TANZANIA, DO AS THE TANZANIANS DO

One thing that fascinated me about the Tanzanian people was their love of Swahili and how they work hard to preserve their language. I was even more fascinated by how they speak; compared with other Swahili-speaking nations, they speak with a lot more rhythm, as though they are singing.

I have come to realise that language is not the only thing Tanzanians take pride in – their food and certain rituals are also important to them.

Just as other countries have their own ways of doing things, so does Tanzania. It's good to understand how things are done so that you don't unintentionally insult someone with what you thought was a lovely gesture. A good example of this is the issue of sniffing food. In the Western world, food is sniffed to inhale the aroma. As positive as this might be in the Western world, this behaviour is frowned on in Tanzania. Sniffing food shows that you are disrespectful and are unsure of the food that has been served to you. Tanzanians believe that food is only sniffed if someone suspects that it is off.

One of my favourite dishes, which is so delicious that it's the national dish of Tanzania, is the creamy, aromatic dish overleaf that is eaten by everyone on the 9th of December (Tanzania's Independence Day).

Maharagwe Ya Nazi

SERVES 4

Beans with Coconut Milk

- Oil for frying (e.g. sunflower oil)
- 1 medium onion, chopped
- 1 large tomato, peeled and chopped
- 2–3 garlic cloves, crushed
- 3 cardamom pods, slightly crushed
- 1 star anise
- 2 whole cloves
- 1 cinnamon stick
- 1 cube vegetable stock
- 1 tsp curry powder
- Salt to taste
- 380 g (2 cups) dried kidney or butter beans, boiled until tender
- 400 ml (1⅔ cups) coconut milk
- 30 g (⅛ cup) granulated sugar (to taste)
- Fresh coriander (cilantro), for garnish

1. Place a saucepan on medium heat and add oil. Add the onion and sauté for about 5 minutes until softened.

2. Add the tomato and cook until tender. Press with a fork to speed up the softening process.

3. Add the garlic, cardamom pods, star anise, cloves, cinnamon stick, vegetable stock, curry powder and salt. Stir for 1 minute.

4. Add the beans to the mixture and cook for about 30 seconds.

5. Pour in the coconut milk and sugar, stir and cover the pan. Cook on medium-low heat, stirring occasionally, until everything is tender (about 20 minutes).

6. Once the flavours are well incorporated, remove the whole spices (star anise, cloves, cardamom pods and cinnamon stick) before serving. Garnish with fresh coriander or coconut milk and enjoy with a food carrier of your choice.

SPICE, RICE AND ALL THINGS NICE

West African countries have their famous jollof rice (also known as thieboudienne or benachin) and in East Africa we have our very own pilau – what I like to call an East Africa show-off/celebration dish. Jollof rice is spicy hot but East African pilau is spicy and flavourful – it takes you straight to spice heaven. Even though pilau was brought to us by the Indians, it has been changed and adapted by the East Africans, and no celebration is complete without it.

Pilau Rice

SERVES 4 AS A MAIN DISH

- 2–3 tbsp grapeseed or other vegetable oil
- 5 g (1 tsp) ground cumin
- 2½ g (½ tsp) ground cardamom
- 2½ g (½ tsp) smoked paprika
- 1¼ g (¼ tsp) curry powder
- 3 whole star anise
- 1 cinnamon stick
- 1 bay leaf
- 1 medium onion, chopped (about 250 g/9 oz)
- 4 garlic cloves, minced
- 2½ g (⅛ oz) minced ginger
- 15–30 g (1–2 tbsp) tomato paste
- 1 small red bell pepper, chopped (about 120 g/4 oz)
- 400 g (14 oz) basmati rice
- 750 ml (3 cups) vegetable stock
- 250 ml (1 cup) coconut milk
- Salt to taste

1. Heat the oil in a large saucepan over medium heat. Add the cumin, cardamom, smoked paprika, curry powder, star anise, cinnamon stick and bay leaf. Stir the spices for 1 minute, releasing their aroma.

2. Add the onion, garlic and ginger. Cook for 1 minute until the onion is translucent.

3. Stir in the tomato paste. Add the red bell pepper and cook for 2–3 minutes until the pepper is tender.

4. Add the rice. Cook for 2 minutes, stirring continuously, coating the rice with the spice mixture.

5. Add the vegetable stock and coconut milk. Season with salt to taste. Bring the mixture to a boil. Reduce heat to low and cover and simmer for 18–20 minutes or until the rice is cooked.

6. Remove the star anise, cinnamon stick and bay leaf. Fluff the rice with a fork. Serve hot.

NOTES:

- Use high-quality basmati rice for best results.
- Pilau rice can be served as a main dish or side accompaniment.

FOOD IN AFRICA

GOING BANANAS!

I admit that I am a bit of a food snob. Not in a picky kind of way, but I love experimenting in the kitchen and I am open to trying new things, as long as they are plant-based. What seems to rub me up the wrong way is when someone confuses one ingredient with another. I tend to forget that not everyone's level of interest in food is the same and that we have not been given the same privilege to discover different foods. I always have to stop myself from correcting people for simply identifying an ingredient incorrectly.

This happens a lot with green bananas and plantains. Each time someone calls a green banana a plantain, my blood pressure rises! I'm not sure if this is because of my snobbish behaviour or whether it's because green bananas are one of my favourite foods on earth. I believe they deserve to stand out and not be overshadowed by the plantain. For the sake of my health, please let's not confuse plantains with green bananas! Yes, they can both be cooked, but they are totally different in size and texture. Also, they both need to shine.

MAD ABOUT MATOKE

Green bananas, popularly known as matoke, are a staple in East African cooking. This is the kind of dish we serve to our visitors in most East African countries such as Rwanda, Burundi, Kenya and Tanzania – and especially Uganda. In fact, Uganda took it to another level, as it is virtually a national ingredient there. Matoke is to Ugandans what chapati is to Kenyans and jollof is to Nigerians. During my time in Uganda, not a day went by that we didn't eat matoke, either for breakfast, lunch or dinner.

NOTES:

- You can use oils such as canola, sunflower or grapeseed as an alternative to coconut oil and olive oil.
- Adjust spice levels according to your taste.
- If fresh garden eggs are unavailable, you can substitute them with eggplant (aubergine).

Green Banana Curry

SERVES 4

- 500 g (1 lb 2 oz) peeled fresh or frozen green bananas
- 2 tbsp coconut oil (or other oil of your choice)
- 1 medium red onion, diced
- 3 garlic cloves, minced
- ½ yellow bell pepper, diced
- ½ green bell pepper, diced
- ½ red bell pepper, diced
- 2 medium tomatoes, diced
- 1 tsp curry powder
- 1 tsp cumin powder
- Salt to taste
- 5 garden eggs (optional), cut into quarters lengthways
- 1 tbsp tomato paste
- 125 ml (½ cup) coconut cream
- 125 ml (½ cup) vegetable stock
- 2 tsp olive oil (or any neutral vegetable oil)
- 200 g (7 oz) mixed mushrooms (oyster and button mushrooms), sliced
- 1 pinch of Italian herbs
- 185 g (1 cup) frozen peas
- Fresh coriander (cilantro), for garnish

1. Cut the green bananas into 2–3 pieces. If using frozen bananas, use them while they are still frozen.
2. In a large saucepan, heat the coconut oil over medium heat. Add the red onion and ⅓ of the garlic. Sauté for 2–3 minutes until the onion is translucent.
3. Stir in all the bell peppers along with the tomatoes. Sauté for an additional 3 minutes until the vegetables soften.
4. Add the curry powder, cumin powder and a pinch of salt. Stir continuously for 1 minute to release the spices' flavours.
5. Add the bananas, garden eggs (if using), tomato paste, coconut cream and vegetable stock. Stir well to combine all the ingredients.
6. Cover the saucepan and allow the curry to simmer for about 20 minutes or until the bananas are tender.
7. In a separate pan, heat the olive oil over medium-high heat. Add the mushrooms and sauté for 5–7 minutes until golden brown.
8. Add the rest of the garlic and the Italian herbs, and cook for another minute. Remove from heat and set aside.
9. After 20 minutes, remove the lid from the banana curry and stir in the peas. Gently fold in the sautéed mushrooms and adjust the seasoning with salt to taste.
10. Serve the curry hot, garnished with fresh coriander. Enjoy with rice, bread or any preferred side.

A SIMPLE ESSENTIAL

I'm always amazed at how sometimes the simple things in life add more value. When I look at chapati ingredients, it astounds me how three simple ingredients have managed to shape East African cuisine forever. You know you have arrived in East Africa when every meal you order in a restaurant comes with a chapati.

Chapati is pan-fried unleavened flatbread that is eaten in almost every country in East Africa, such as Burundi, Uganda, Rwanda, Tanzania and Kenya. Chapatis are a very big part of East African cuisine because they serve as food carriers. In many instances they are used as bases to support other dishes and add balance to every meal. This means they accompany stews, dips, sauces, soups and other side dishes, and are eaten daily.

East African chapatis, however, are different from Indian chapatis. East African chapatis are made with white bread flour and are coiled up and have oil in them. The purpose of the coil is to create layers within the chapatis and to help them become light and flaky. As you pan-fry them you lightly brush the outer layer with a little oil, giving them a crispy edge.

NOTES:

- Use high-gluten flour such as bread flour for a soft and pliable dough.
- Ensure that the water is warm but not scalding to avoid cooking the flour.
- Adjust the cooking time based on the heat of your stove; each chapati should puff up and become golden brown.
- Use a standard mixer if you don't want to do a workout!

Chapatis

MAKES 10–15

Unleavened Wheat Flatbread

375 g (3 cups) bread flour (high-gluten flour recommended), plus extra for kneading and dusting

1 tsp salt

4 tbsp grapeseed or other vegetable oil, plus extra for brushing

375 ml (1½ cups) warm water (not too hot to touch)

1. In a large bowl, combine the flour and salt. Add the oil and 250 ml (1 cup) warm water. Mix until the dough starts to come together.
2. Gradually add more warm water (up to 375 ml/1½ cups total) as needed, until the dough is soft but not sticky.
3. Transfer the dough to a flat surface. Knead for about 10 minutes, adding flour if the dough is too sticky, until it is smooth and elastic.
4. Place the dough back in the bowl, cover with a damp cloth and let it rest for 15 minutes at room temperature.
5. After resting, divide the dough into 10–15 equal portions and roll each portion into a ball. Place the balls on a floured surface and cover with a cloth. Let them rest for 10 minutes.
6. Take one dough ball and roll it out into a rough circle about 15–20 cm (6–8 inches) in diameter. The shape doesn't need to be perfect at this stage.
7. Lightly brush the surface with a little oil, then roll the dough into a log, as if you were rolling up a scroll. Coil the log into a spiral shape (like a cinnamon roll), place it on a tray and cover with a cloth. Repeat with the remaining dough balls. Let the coiled dough rest for another 10–15 minutes at room temperature.
8. After resting, gently flatten the coiled dough into a circle with your hands or a rolling pin. This helps create the soft layers in the chapati when cooked.
9. Heat a pan over medium heat until hot. Place the rolled chapati in the pan and cook for about 30 seconds or until you see bubbles forming on the surface.
10. Flip the chapati and cook the other side for another 30 seconds until golden brown. You can press it gently with a spatula to help it puff up.
11. Optionally, brush with a little oil while cooking for added flavour. Repeat with each dough ball until all the chapatis are cooked.
12. Keep the cooked chapatis warm by covering them with a cloth. Serve them warm with your favourite dish.

WHAT ARE GREEN BANANAS?

African Highland bananas, commonly known as matoke or igitoki across East Africa, are a cultivated starchy green banana originating from the African Great Lakes. Unlike fruity ripe sweet bananas, matoke are harvested green and cooked as a starch or food carrier before they are ripe.

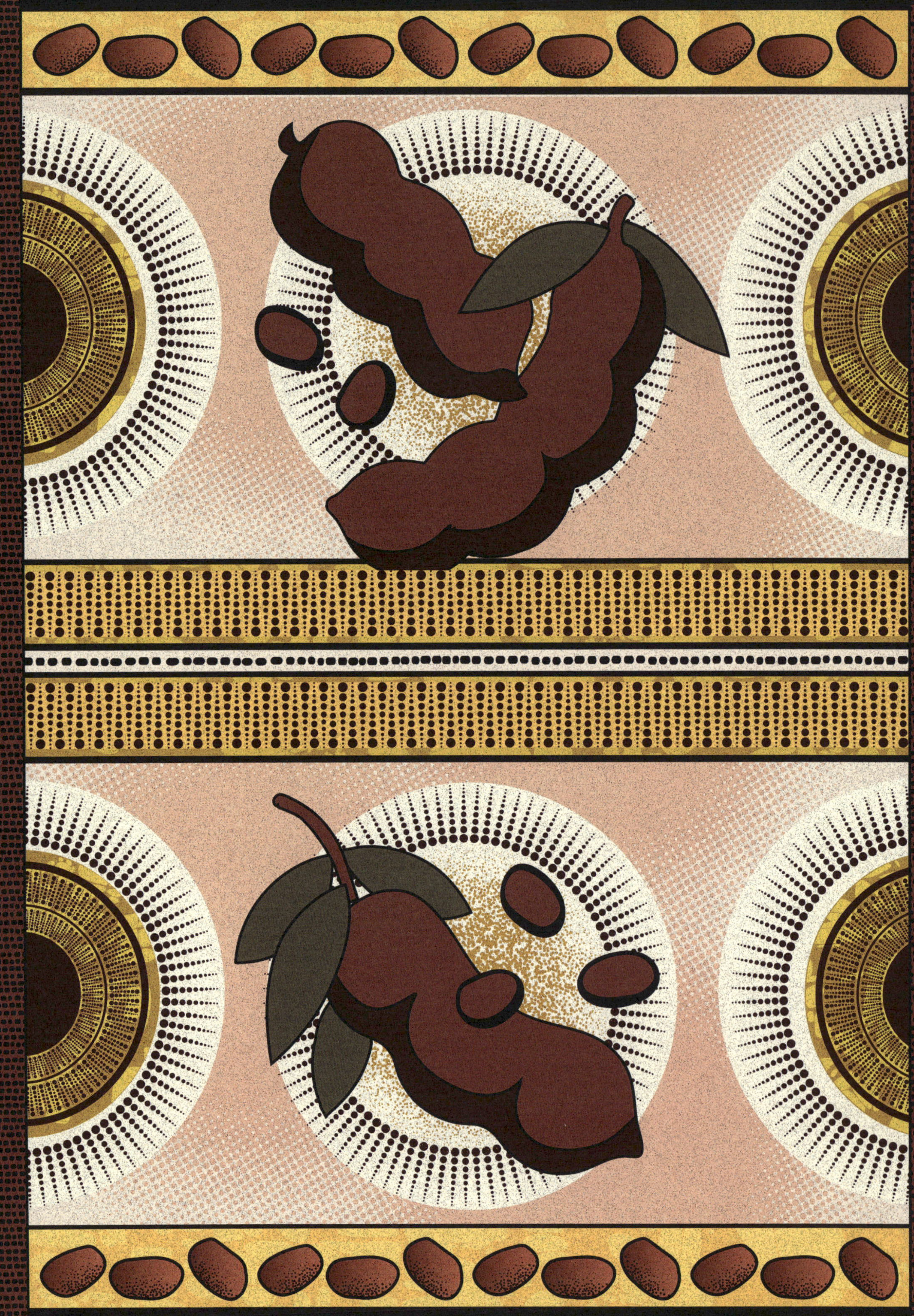

KENYA

FIVE

TEATIME IS CHAI TIME

Tea drinking is a very big part of East African culture, especially in Kenya, where Kenyan people welcome visitors with a cup of chai. In East Africa, the word chai doesn't mean a specific type of tea, it's a name given to all types of teas. We normally serve chai with mandazi or, as they are widely known, African doughnuts. Kenyans are also known to observe a tradition of afternoon teatime, which was introduced during colonial times, and spiced mandazi are the perfect accompaniment to a cup of chai.

As I went down memory lane when compiling the recipes in this book, I was reminded of all the flavours in mandazi, and their soft texture as I dipped them in a cup of hot tea as a child. I was also reminded of one of my childhood chores. When I was growing up in Kenya, it was my daily duty to take an empty milk container with me to school. On my way home from school I would pass by one of the homes where cows were kept. We had an arrangement with the people living there that we could collect milk daily and my mother would pay them monthly.

As I sat and waited for my milk, I loved watching the owner invite the cow into the place where she sat and then start milking. Thanks to the fresh milk and Kenyan-grown tea, the tea I drank in Kenya had a depth and deliciousness to it that was different from any other teas I have drunk outside that country.

What many people don't know is that Kenya exports a lot of tea – almost as much as the biggest tea exporters we know such as China, Sri Lanka and India.

I have since stopped drinking cow's milk in my tea, but Kenyan-grown tea is still my first choice when it comes to tea. Afternoon teatime might be a British tradition, but Kenyans have given it their own twist with their special brand of African hospitality.

Chai Tea

SERVES 4

Milky Tea Cooked with Aromatic Spices

- 8 cardamom pods
- 8 cloves
- 4 allspice berries
- 1–2 cinnamon sticks
- 2 star anise
- 2½ cm (1-inch) piece of fresh ginger, sliced
- 500 ml (2 cups) plant milk of your choice
- 1 tsp vanilla extract
- 1 tbsp loose tea (Kenyan black tea or rooibos tea)
- 500 ml (2 cups) water
- Sweetener of your choice (sugar, agave, etc.) to taste

1. Use a mortar or heavy object to squash the cardamom pods. This helps release their flavour.
2. In a saucepan over medium heat, combine the cardamom, cloves, allspice, cinnamon sticks, star anise and ginger.
3. Add the milk and vanilla extract to the saucepan. Allow the mixture to simmer gently for about 5–10 minutes, letting the spices infuse.
4. Once the milk mixture is heated, add the loose tea and water to the saucepan. Increase the heat and bring the mixture to a boil, watching carefully to prevent it from boiling over.
5. Once boiling, remove the saucepan from the heat and strain the tea into cups using a fine-mesh strainer.
6. Add your sweetener of choice to taste while the tea is still warm, stirring until dissolved.

ICED CHAI TEA

Additional ingredients

- Ice cubes
- Vegan whipped cream (optional, for topping)

1. Follow the same steps to make the hot chai tea. Once strained and sweetened, allow the chai to cool to room temperature, or refrigerate until chilled.
2. Fill a glass with ice cubes and pour the chilled chai over the ice. Top with a dollop of vegan whipped cream if desired.
3. Serve immediately.

NOTES:

- Adjust the amount of sweetener according to your taste. You can also customise the spice levels according to your preference.
- Experiment with different plant milks such as almond, oat or coconut for varied flavours.

AFRICAN HOSPITALITY

Hospitality is inextricably intertwined with being an African. Kindness to strangers is considered a great virtue on the African continent and I love how we Africans are so courteous and welcoming to strangers. Greeting a stranger is done with care and without rushing. It is not a mere formality; rather, the host takes the time to express sincerity and interest. The stranger is also viewed as a "bringer of news". Many questions are asked about the places and people that they left, as well as those they encountered en route.

Even if the host has little, they will always offer their guests the best they have. Whenever we had guests at our home in Kenya, I would watch my mom go all out to get the tea ready for guests or get us to do it while she caught up with the visitors.

Our home was a place where all strangers and visitors would come for free accommodation. We saw people come in and out of our home – enough to fill a stadium – and the treatment was always the same.

My family took pride in being hospitable, but I noticed that hospitality went both ways. Most people feel that it's important to take a gift when they visit someone's home. In turn, the host believes that guests deserve to be welcomed with a meal. As children, we always looked forward to the amazing gifts we would receive from the strangers who stayed in our home. Since it is an insult to refuse gifts or food in Africa, let's just say that we had no choice but to accept with a smile even those that we didn't really like. Being a great host was instilled in me, and I also always give my guests something for the road when they leave. One of my favourite things to give is a blend of spices for tea that we used to drink at home – with my own twist.

Chai Blend

MAKES ABOUT 250 G (1 CUP) OF BLEND

- 200 g (7 oz) soya milk powder
- 2 tbsp coconut blossom sugar (or sweetener of your choice)
- 1 tbsp red espresso powder (or your preferred tea/coffee powder)
- 1 tsp vanilla powder
- 1 tsp ground cardamom
- 2 tsp ground allspice
- 2 tsp ground cinnamon
- 2 tsp ground cloves
- 6 tsp ground ginger

1. Combine all the ingredients in a large bowl. Stir the mixture well until everything is evenly combined.

2. Transfer the chai blend to an airtight spice container or jar. Store it in a cool, dry place to keep it fresh.

3. For a single serving, use 1 tbsp of the chai blend. Mix it with 250 ml (1 cup) of hot water or your choice of hot dairy-free milk. Stir well to combine.

4. Taste your chai and add more sweetener if desired, but the blend should be sweet enough on its own.

NOTES:

- You can adjust the amount of each spice to suit your flavour preferences.
- For a creamier chai, try using oat or almond milk instead of soya milk.
- This blend can be used in various recipes, such as for smoothies or baked goods, for added flavour.

BITTERSWEET MEMORIES AND MANDAZI

Food often evokes precious memories of our loved ones, connecting us to moments that stay with us forever. My life has been shaped by many memories, some filled with joy and others with sorrow. One memory from my past, during the turmoil in my home country, stands out the most. In 1994, when violence escalated and we fled the country, my family found refuge in Goma in the DRC.

It was a chaotic time, with so much suffering around us. Despite this, we were fortunate to find shelter with a kind pastor who welcomed us into his compound. One day my cousin Jeanne and I, in our childlike innocence, tried to escape the grim reality for just a moment. With some money (I can't even remember where it came from) we went to go and buy mandazi – a small comfort amid the turmoil.

We slipped out of the compound and walked through the streets, passing heartbreaking scenes of people who had lost everything. But our focus was on finding mandazi, a little treat we both loved. When we finally found some, we ignored everything else and simply enjoyed our food, excited for just a moment of normalcy.

However, soon after that Jeanne started feeling unwell. I panicked and called for my older sister Charlotte as I held Jeanne in my arms. Sadly, by the time Charlotte arrived, Jeanne was slipping away. It's unclear what exactly caused her to fall ill, and while some thought the food might have been contaminated, I've never been sure.

That day, at just nine years old, I learnt how fragile life is. Though I lost many loved ones that year, the memories I hold closest are the ones tied to moments of shared meals and the joy they brought us. Jeanne's passing was a heartbreaking moment, but I choose to remember her smile and the excitement we shared about mandazi. Now, when I make it, it's a way of honouring her memory, reminding me of the love and joy that food can bring, even in the toughest times.

Mandazi

MAKES ABOUT 12

East African Doughnuts

- 200 ml (scant 1 cup) canned coconut milk, warmed
- 100 g (½ cup) granulated sugar
- 2 tsp active dry yeast
- 1 tbsp flax meal
- 3 tbsp water
- 450 g (3⅓ cups) bread flour, plus extra as needed
- 1 tsp ground cardamom
- 1 tsp grated nutmeg
- 50 g (1 cup) coconut flakes
- 1 tsp salt
- Vegetable oil for deep-frying (e.g. sunflower oil)
- Icing sugar (confectioners' sugar) for sprinkling

1. In a large bowl, combine the coconut milk, sugar and yeast. Set aside for 5 minutes until frothy.

2. In a small bowl, mix the flax meal with the water to make a flax "egg". Let it sit for a few minutes to thicken.

3. In another large bowl (or a stand mixer), add half the flour, the cardamom, nutmeg, coconut flakes and salt. Mix well.

4. Add the flax "egg" to the yeast mixture and stir to combine. Pour the wet mixture into the bowl with the dry ingredients. Mix until well combined.

5. Gradually add the remaining flour and knead the dough by hand or in a stand mixer for about 10 minutes or until smooth and elastic. Add more flour if the dough is too sticky.

6. Place the dough in a greased bowl, turning it to coat. Cover loosely with a clean cloth and let it rise in a warm place for 1–2 hours or until doubled in size.

7. Once risen, roll out the dough to about 2½ cm (1 inch) thick. Cut into bite-sized pieces or triangles.

8. Pour vegetable oil into a large saucepan to a depth of at least 7½ cm (3 inches) and heat over medium until hot. Carefully add the mandazi pieces to the hot oil and fry until golden brown (about 3–5 minutes, depending on their size). Fry in batches if necessary, and turn each mandazi once.

9. Remove the mandazi and drain on paper towels. Sprinkle with icing sugar, serve on a plate and enjoy with chai tea.

NOTES:

- Test the oil by dropping a bit of dough into it. If it sizzles, the oil is hot enough and the mandazi won't absorb too much oil.
- Add more cardamom or nutmeg for a stronger flavour.

AN APPETITE FOR POTATOES

I'm always ready to talk about potatoes. I have never seen a vegetable as satisfying as these tubers, and for someone who prefers savoury over sweet, street food simply wouldn't be the same without them. Potatoes make plant-based living so much easier. They can be healthy, they can be "junky", they can be anything you want them to be. Hence, in my world, potatoes are the best vegetable you can get.

I can't mention potatoes without talking about my favourite street food in Africa, viazi karai, which is synonymous with the coast of Kenya. Not only are they a favourite among tourists, they are also popular among the local community. Children buy them on the pavement on their way home from school and adults love them just as much. It's difficult to pass by someone selling them without checking to see if you have enough coins in your pocket to buy some! These delicious batter-coated fried potatoes are sold everywhere from street corners to hotels and restaurants. You can eat them on their own, but they are best served with tamarind sauce (p. 113).

Viazi Karai

SERVES 5

Crispy Fried Potatoes

- 5–10 medium-sized potatoes, peeled
- 2 garlic cloves, minced
- 2 sprigs of fresh rosemary
- Salt and black pepper
- 1 tsp chilli powder (optional, for spice)
- Juice of 3 lemons
- 350 g (3 cups) plain (all-purpose) flour or cake flour
- Small bunch of fresh coriander (cilantro), finely chopped
- Pinch of turmeric
- 2 tsp garlic powder
- 1 tsp onion powder
- 150 ml (⅔ cup) water (adjust as needed for batter consistency)
- Vegetable oil for deep-frying (e.g. sunflower oil)

1. In a pot, add the potatoes with enough water to cover them, then add the minced garlic, rosemary and salt and pepper to taste.
2. Bring to a boil over medium heat and cook the potatoes until just tender. Do not overcook them. Drain the potatoes and let them cool.
3. In a small bowl, mix the chilli powder (if using), a pinch of salt and the lemon juice. Slice each boiled potato in half and spread a bit of this mixture inside. Reassemble the potatoes and set aside.
4. In a large bowl, mix the flour, coriander, turmeric, garlic powder, onion powder and a pinch of salt.
5. Gradually add the water, stirring continuously, until the mixture reaches the consistency of thick pancake batter.
6. Heat oil in a deep frying pan over medium-high heat (enough oil to fully submerge the potatoes).
7. Once the oil is hot, dip each potato into the batter, ensuring it's fully coated. The two halves will stick together because of the batter. Fry the battered potatoes in the hot oil until they are golden brown and crispy (about 3–4 minutes per side).
8. Remove from the oil and drain on paper towels.
9. Serve hot with tamarind sauce for an authentic Mombasa experience.

Tamarind Sauce

MAKES 250 ML (1 CUP)

- Boiling water (enough to soak the dates)
- 100 g (3½ oz) dates, pitted
- 100 g (3½ oz) tamarind paste
- 1 tsp cumin powder
- Salt to taste
- 1 tsp lemon juice

1. In a bowl, pour the boiling water over the dates and let them sit for about 10 minutes until softened.

2. In a blender, add the soaked dates and about half a cup (125 ml) of the water used to soak them, the tamarind paste, cumin powder and salt.

3. Blend until smooth. For a smoother texture, pass the mixture through a fine-mesh sieve, but this step is optional.

4. Transfer the mixture to a saucepan and simmer over low heat for 8–10 minutes, stirring occasionally to prevent burning, until the sauce thickens.

5. Remove from heat, stir in the lemon juice and let the sauce cool before storing in a jar or sauce container.

NOTE:

- You can also use whole tamarind. Break open 250 g (1 cup) whole tamarind pods and remove the outer shell, leaving just the pulp and seeds. Combine the tamarind pulp and seeds with 500 ml (2 cups) water in a bowl. Let it soak for 4–6 hours or overnight. Strain the mixture through cheesecloth or a fine-mesh sieve into a bowl. Squeeze the pulp to extract as much liquid as possible. Discard the solids. Reduce on the stove and allow to cool.

SEASONS' TEACHINGS

When my brother and I moved to Kenya to live with our new dad (my uncle) it was the most awkward time of my life. I felt so out of place. Apart from being in a new country and new environment, one of the things that made my life difficult was the fact that I couldn't speak a word of English or Swahili. You can imagine how the first day of school was for my brother and me when other children saw two foreign children who couldn't speak. However, as the days went by, we started to learn Swahili, and we adapted.

It was hard to make friends, but one of the things that kept me going was food. During this time, I learnt how to make chapati and the popular sukuma wiki (collard greens), which translates to "stretching the week". Through my experience in Kenya I learnt that no season is wasted; good things come out of bad days and better things are born out of bad experiences. I learnt to use the uncomfortable times in my life to do things I have control over and leave everything else to take care of itself. Once the season is over, there is a realisation that something beautiful came out of it.

During this season I perfected my sukuma-cutting skills. In Kenya, cutting sukuma wiki was a skill that required mastering; the greens needed to be finely cut at a high speed without cutting oneself.

Collard greens can be found in the simplest gardens in East Africa. They are so common that even the poor can afford to eat them in abundance. Since these greens are available all year round, they form part of the East African staple diet; no one can go for a week without eating sukuma wiki, especially in Kenya and Tanzania.

People have therefore developed different ways to prepare them, from the most affordable and simple recipes to complicated ones. Preparing them is not that difficult, but cutting them to perfection into the smallest possible size requires training, and I used all the free time I had to perfect this skill.

Sukuma Wiki

SERVES 4 AS A SIDE DISH

Sautéed Collard Greens and Spinach

- 2–3 tbsp grapeseed or other vegetable oil
- 1 large white onion, finely chopped
- 1–2 tsp minced garlic (adjust to taste)
- 3 medium tomatoes, diced
- 1 tbsp paprika
- Salt to taste
- 2 bunches of collard greens (about 500 g/1 lb 2 oz), finely chopped
- 1 bunch of spinach (about 250 g/9 oz), finely chopped (not baby spinach; look for large leaves similar to Swiss chard)

1. Heat the oil in a medium-large saucepan over medium heat. Add the onion and sauté until it becomes soft and translucent (about 3–4 minutes).
2. Add the garlic and continue sautéing for an additional 2 minutes, stirring frequently to avoid burning.
3. Stir in the tomatoes, paprika and salt. Continue cooking for about 2 minutes, stirring occasionally, until the tomatoes soften and the flavours begin to blend.
4. Add the collard greens, cover the saucepan and let them steam for about 2 minutes. Uncover the pan, stir the greens and continue cooking for another 2 minutes.
5. Add the spinach to the saucepan, stirring it into the mixture. Continue cooking for 5–10 more minutes, stirring occasionally, until the greens are tender but still bright green and slightly crunchy. Taste and adjust salt if necessary.
6. Remove from heat and serve immediately with ugali (a staple East African dish made from maize flour) or your preferred side dish.

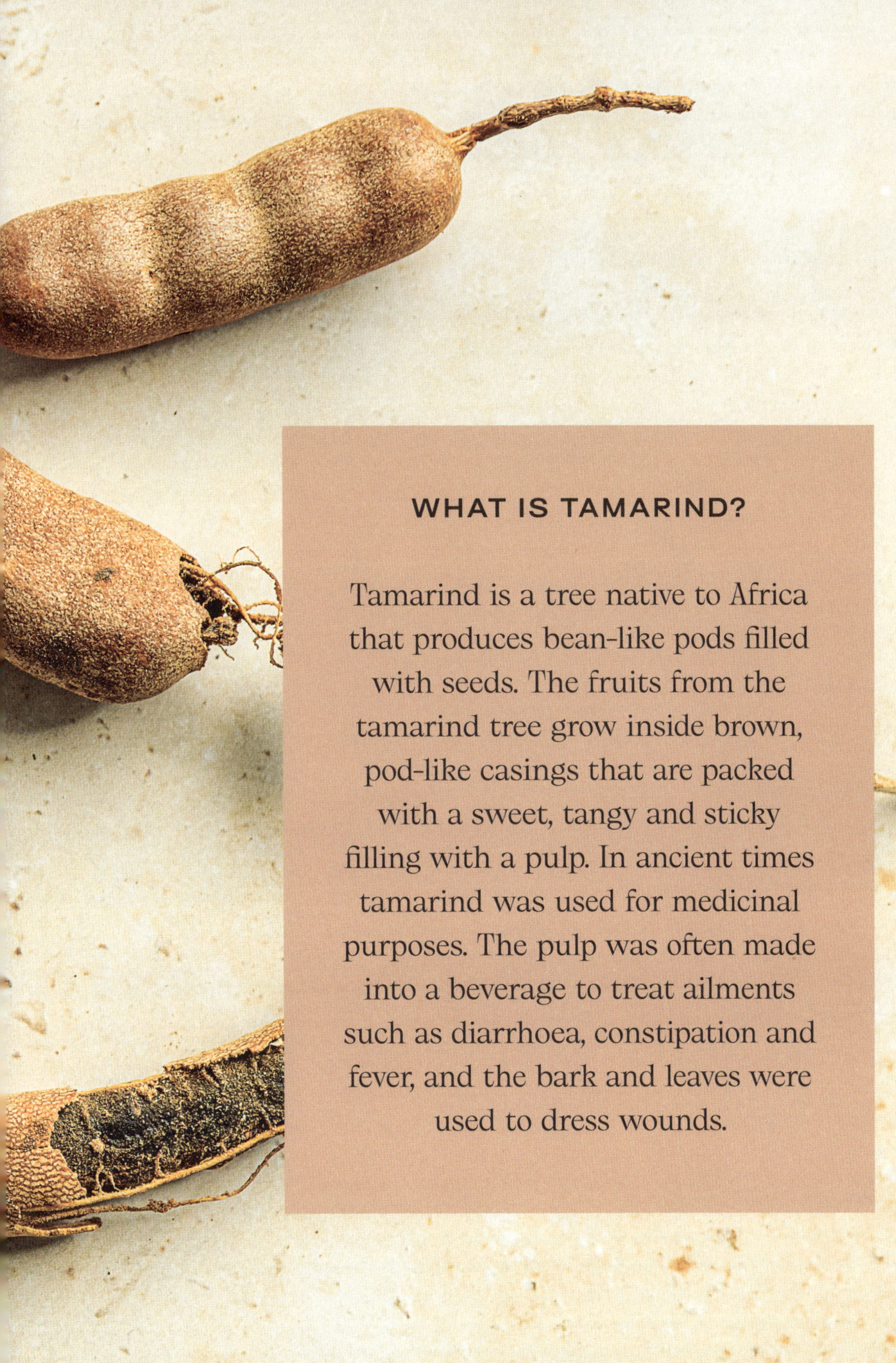

WHAT IS TAMARIND?

Tamarind is a tree native to Africa that produces bean-like pods filled with seeds. The fruits from the tamarind tree grow inside brown, pod-like casings that are packed with a sweet, tangy and sticky filling with a pulp. In ancient times tamarind was used for medicinal purposes. The pulp was often made into a beverage to treat ailments such as diarrhoea, constipation and fever, and the bark and leaves were used to dress wounds.

RWANDA

SIX

COUNTRY OF A THOUSAND HILLS AND SMILES

When we talk about African hospitality, we are not simply talking about the process of inviting and entertaining guests. In Africa, it's about Ubuntu, a quality that includes the essential human virtues of compassion and humanity. It's a core part of our identity. It has been ingrained in the fabric of our communities, it's our moral code and it's seen in how we eat and share food. There is an African proverb that says, "One who eats alone cannot discuss the taste of food with others." We often simplify our meals so that they are easy to prepare and will be readily available in case a stranger happens to pass by.

In Rwandan homes, guests have a way of showing up unannounced. It's part of cultural politeness to serve your guests something to eat because you don't know where they have been or if they have had something to eat. Most Rwandan dishes are extremely simple. They are cooked in their own natural flavours without additional spices and are simply seasoned with salt. This uncomplicated process allows the host to spend time with their guests.

Rwanda is well known as a country of a thousand hills. What captivates visitors to the heart of Africa most is the smiles on the faces of the people they meet. The last person I spoke to who had visited Rwanda said, "They should call it a country with a thousand smiles because the smiles outnumber the hills."

Dishes like the cabbage recipe overleaf are popular because they're easy to make and can be prepared quickly for guests.

Amashu Akaranze

SERVES 4 AS A SIDE DISH

East African Cabbage

- 2 tbsp grapeseed or other vegetable oil
- 1 large red onion, diced
- 3 garlic cloves, minced
- 1 tsp curry powder (optional)
- 530 g (about 6 cups) finely chopped cabbage (from 1 medium head)
- 1 cup grated carrots
- 1 cup crushed or chopped tomatoes (fresh or canned)
- Salt and black pepper to taste

1. Heat the oil in a large saucepan over medium heat. Add the onion and sauté until soft and translucent (about 3–4 minutes).

2. Add the garlic and curry powder (if using), and cook for another 1 minute, stirring frequently to avoid burning.

3. Add the cabbage, carrots and tomatoes to the pan. Sprinkle a pinch of salt and freshly ground black pepper over the vegetables. Cover the pan and let the vegetables steam for about 1 minute.

4. Stir the vegetables well after steaming and continue cooking uncovered for 8–10 minutes, stirring occasionally, until the cabbage is tender but still slightly crunchy. Adjust the cooking time based on your preferred level of tenderness.

5. Remove from heat and serve warm as a side dish to accompany your main meal.

UNFORGOTTEN FLAVOURS

After my three siblings and I had been in the refugee camp in the DRC for about two years, my cousin Emanuel picked us up to meet our uncle's friend Safari, who came to fetch one of my brothers and me so that we could be reunited with my uncle Shamba. Although I was sad to be leaving our older siblings behind, I was still incredibly excited, as I couldn't wait to leave the refugee camp. We had one week to prepare for the trip and everywhere I went, I spread the news that I was going to live with my uncle in faraway Kenya.

I started to imagine how life would be out of the refugee camp. The thought of never having to fetch water again was enough to make me excited. I thought of the likelihood of having plenty of food and this meant there wouldn't be days when we would go to bed hungry. What's more, the idea of being in a new place and having a new beginning was enough for me to count all the sleeps in anticipation of the week being over.

Emanuel came to get us, we met up with Safari and headed with him to Kampala in Uganda, where he stayed with his family. The plan was to stay with them until my uncle came to get us. The morning after we arrived, a milkman came with cassava fried chips dipped in masala sauce. I don't know what was in that sauce, but those were the best masala mogo I had ever tasted. Admittedly, they were also the first I had ever tasted.

In Rwanda, we used to cook cassava roots by simply boiling them in bean water and serve them with beans and salt. When I went to Uganda, suddenly cassava became a delicious breakfast treat, which I used to look forward to every morning. When we were in Uganda, my brother and I didn't go to school because we were waiting for my uncle to come and get us. The only motivation to get up early every morning, besides waiting for my uncle, was to sit outside and wait for the milkman while eating mogo. I have tried to re-create this East African treat even though I don't think it will ever come close to the one I ate as a child in Uganda.

Masala Mogo

SERVES 4

Spicy Cassava

- 500 g (1 lb 2 oz) cassava (fresh or frozen, both work)
- Salt
- Vegetable oil for deep-frying (e.g. sunflower oil), plus 1 tbsp for masala sauce
- 200 ml (scant 1 cup) tomato puree
- 1 tsp onion powder
- 1 tsp garlic powder
- 1 tsp ground cumin
- 1 tsp ground coriander
- 1 tbsp granulated sugar
- 1 tbsp lemon juice
- Freshly chopped coriander, for garnish
- Lemon wedges (optional)

1. If using fresh cassava, peel and cut it into large chunks. If using frozen cassava, you can use it as is.
2. In a large pot, add the cassava and enough water to cover it, plus a pinch of salt. Bring the water to a boil and cook the cassava until tender but not overcooked (about 15–20 minutes). Drain the water and let the cassava cool down.
3. Once the cassava has cooled, cut it into chip-like pieces (fry-sized strips).
4. Heat the oil in a large frying pan or deep fryer over medium heat. Fry the cassava chips until they are crispy and golden brown (about 4–5 minutes per batch). Drain on paper towels and set aside.
5. In a separate pan, heat 1 tbsp of oil over medium heat. Add the tomato puree and cook for about 2 minutes.
6. Stir in the onion powder, garlic powder, cumin and coriander. Cook for an additional minute, stirring continuously.
7. Add the sugar, lemon juice and salt to taste. Mix well and cook for another minute until the sauce thickens.
8. Add the fried cassava chips to the pan with the masala sauce and toss to coat the cassava evenly with the sauce.
9. Sprinkle chopped coriander on top. Squeeze the lemon wedges over them for an extra burst of flavour. Serve hot with a dip of your choice (e.g. vegan mayo)

"SOUPER" FOOD FOR THE SOUL

I was physically fragile and sickly as a child; this also meant that I was a picky eater, and eating was not exactly one of my favourite things. I ate because food kept me alive. My mama would always mix as many vegetables as possible together and blend them into a soup. That way, even if I ended up eating only once a day, I would at least have eaten something nutritious. This was my way of life for the early years of my existence. I can't honestly say that I enjoyed the soups I ate when I was growing up, but they hold great memories for me. They were a way for my mama to keep me alive.

As I grew older and started making food for myself and for others, I started to associate soup with wellness, care, sustenance and love. I have not only perfected the art of making delicious soups but I have also made it my own way of saying "I love you" and "I care about you". Just as my mama used soup to keep me alive, I use it to show others how much I love them by feeding them this comforting and nourishing food, especially when they are unwell.

Butternut soup has always been my go-to soup. Recently, I decided to go back in time and make pumpkin soup. I grew up eating pumpkins. One of my favourite parts of pumpkin days in our household was when, after my mama had prepared the pumpkins, she would dry and roast the seeds for us to eat as snacks. Everything about my mama's cooking was marked with love. These are the memories I still have of her.

This soup is not only my comfort on cold winter days and a boost when I feel worn down. It is the very dish that keeps my late mama's memories in my heart, and I wanted to share it with you.

Isupu Yibihaza

SERVES 4

Pumpkin Soup

- 1.2 kg (2.6 lb) pumpkin (butternut squash or similar can also work), peeled, seeds removed and cut into 4 cm (1½-inch) chunks
- 2 tbsp olive or other vegetable oil
- Salt and pepper
- 1 onion, sliced
- 3 garlic cloves, peeled
- 15 g (½ oz) fresh ginger, peeled and roughly chopped
- 1 tsp paprika
- 1 tsp cumin
- 750 ml (3 cups) vegetable stock
- 250 ml (1 cup) water
- 185 ml (¾ cup) coconut cream
- Fresh coriander (cilantro) or chilli flakes, for garnish
- Roasted pumpkin seeds, for garnish

1. Preheat the oven to 180 °C (350 °F).

2. Toss the pumpkin chunks with 1 tbsp of oil and a pinch of salt. Spread the pumpkin evenly on a baking sheet and roast for about 30 minutes or until soft and tender. Check tenderness with a knife.

3. While the pumpkin is roasting, heat the remaining oil in a large saucepan over medium heat. Add the onion and sauté for about 2 minutes until softened. Add the garlic, ginger, paprika and cumin, and sauté for another minute until fragrant.

4. Pour in the vegetable stock and water, and bring the mixture to a boil.

5. Once the pumpkin is roasted, add it to the saucepan along with the coconut cream. (Reserve a little for garnish.) Let the soup simmer for 5 minutes to allow the flavours to combine.

6. Use a stick blender to blend the soup until smooth or carefully transfer the mixture in batches to a stand blender and blend until smooth. Return the blended soup to the saucepan. Season with salt and pepper to taste.

7. Ladle the soup into bowls, drizzle with the reserved coconut cream and garnish with the coriander or chilli flakes and pumpkin seeds.

HARVEST RHYTHM

I recently attended a Rwandan wedding in Cape Town. I hadn't been to a wedding in a while, so I didn't know what to expect. The ceremony started, the elders completed all the formalities and finally it was time for food. What I love about African weddings is that we don't compromise when it comes to food. We make enough so that those mamas who want to keep some in their bags can still have extra to eat during the wedding reception.

There is something wonderful that usually happens after the food. The DJ will start to play a traditional song, and this always happens, as if it is a written rule in the Rwandan DJ community. After that, people will get up one by one and head to the dance floor, some of them already singing. From what I know, most of these dances are not planned as part of the programme, but the way they are so perfectly put together in terms of choreography makes it seem as though everyone on the guest list was invited to a rehearsal I didn't know about. These dances are so integrated into who we are that the dancing just happens spontaneously. I couldn't think of a better way of communicating a sense of appreciation to the host while reflecting a sense of community than through rhythm.

Apparently, this type of impromptu singing and dancing happens at harvest time to keep workers excited and motivated. I can only imagine how wonderful this is during the harvesting of sorghum, beans and tea, which are some of the biggest crops grown in Rwanda.

Salade Y'amasaka

SERVES 4–6

Sorghum Salad

- 750 ml–1 litre (3–4 cups) water (or more if needed)
- 150 g (5½ oz) sorghum grains, washed
- Salt
- 200 g (7 oz) fresh flat-leaf parsley, chopped
- 70 g (2½ oz) fresh mint leaves, chopped
- 1 medium red onion, finely diced
- 1 garlic clove, minced
- 1 medium cucumber, diced
- 150 g (1 cup) grape tomatoes, halved
- ½ medium pineapple, peeled and cut into small cubes
- 30 g (1 oz) dried cranberries
- 2 tbsp avocado oil (or olive oil)
- 2 tbsp lemon juice
- 1 tsp garlic and herb seasoning

1. In a medium saucepan, bring the water to a boil. Add the sorghum and a pinch of salt.
2. Reduce the heat to medium-low, cover and simmer for about 1 hour or until the sorghum is tender, creamy and fully cooked.
3. Check halfway through to ensure there's enough water, adding more if necessary to prevent the sorghum from drying out.
4. Once cooked, drain any excess water and set the sorghum aside to cool. Cooking sorghum ahead of time helps to speed up the salad preparation.
5. In a large mixing bowl, combine the parsley, mint, red onion, garlic, cucumber, tomatoes, pineapple and dried cranberries.
6. In a small bowl, whisk together the avocado oil, lemon juice and the garlic and herb seasoning, and salt to taste.
7. Once the sorghum has cooled, add it to the salad mixture. Pour the dressing over the salad and gently toss to combine everything.
8. For the best flavour, let the salad sit for about an hour at room temperature before serving to allow the flavours to meld together.

A LOVE AFFAIR WITH POTATOES

I have many fond memories of my childhood, and one of my favourites is a trip to the village of Ruhengeri to visit our grandparents. The village was relatively cold because of the surrounding volcanic mountains. Nevertheless, it was the most beautiful place in the world – extraordinarily green and full of life. Food was also very different from what we were used to in the city and that made it exciting.

I loved the uncomplicated nature of our grandparents' meals. They would only season meals with salt and would allow the natural flavours of the ingredients to come through. That's how an ingredient like a potato would take centre stage.

One of the things I looked forward to was evening storytelling time in my grandparents' small outside kitchen. We would gather around the fire as my grandmother cooked while she told us stories. She gave each of us a potato to roast in the same fire she cooked on, and it seemed as though potatoes were everywhere in that village. People ate them boiled, roasted in the fire or cooked in bean water. It was those experiences that started my love affair with potatoes. I love their heartiness, but I believe I eat them from a place of memory more than anything. There isn't a week that passes without me indulging in a potato dish.

Ibirayi Byokeje Mu Ifuru

SERVES 4 AS A SIDE DISH

Roast Potatoes

- 60 ml (¼ cup) grapeseed or other vegetable oil
- 2 garlic cloves, minced
- 1 tbsp onion powder
- 1 tsp smoked paprika
- 1 tbsp freshly chopped rosemary
- 1 tbsp freshly chopped parsley
- 1 tbsp fresh thyme leaves
- Salt
- Freshly ground black pepper
- 500 g (1 lb 2 oz) baby potatoes, halved

1. Preheat the oven to 180 °C (350 °F).
2. In a large mixing bowl, combine the oil, garlic, onion powder, smoked paprika, rosemary, parsley and thyme, and season with salt and black pepper to taste. Mix well to create a flavourful herb mixture.
3. Add the potatoes to the bowl. Toss them in the herb mixture, ensuring they are evenly coated.
4. Spread the seasoned potatoes out in a single layer on a baking tray, making sure they are spaced apart for even cooking.
5. Bake for 35–40 minutes or until the potatoes are golden brown and fork-tender. Turn the potatoes halfway through the cooking time for even browning.
6. Remove from the oven and let them cool slightly before serving. Enjoy your delicious roast potatoes as a side dish.

UNITED BY FOOD

I grew up eating igihembe, which is a delicious Rwandan bean stew. There is quite a process involved in preparing this dish. This includes soaking the beans for at least three hours and peeling one bean at a time until all the skins have been removed. Peeling the beans was a communal task – something the whole family got involved in. This became a catch-up moment for most children and their parents. While sitting peeling beans you had time to find out what everyone was up to, and it was also a good way for everyone to get involved in the preparation of their meal.

We now live in a fast-paced society. We no longer live as a community, so making igihembe is not that common any more. I imagine that not many people have the time to peel soaked beans, but I do it while watching a series on Netflix. In this way I don't feel as though I have been unproductive while watching TV for hours. This process is super therapeutic, so I make attempts to go back to my childhood by peeling beans. I don't only make stew, I also make fried bean patties for my quick bean burger nights.

Burger Y'ibishyimbo

MAKES 4 BURGERS

Bean Burgers

- 180 g (6 oz) dried black-eyed beans
- 1 small red onion, finely chopped
- 3 garlic cloves, minced
- 2 medium Scotch bonnet peppers, seeds removed and sliced
- 1 red bell pepper, chopped
- 1 vegetable bouillon cube
- Fresh coriander (cilantro), finely chopped
- Salt to taste
- 750 ml (3 cups) oil for frying (e.g. sunflower oil)
- 4 buns of your choice
- 4 lettuce leaves
- Tomato, sliced
- Vegan (chilli) mayonnaise (optional)
- Tomato sauce (optional)
- Caramelised onions (optional)

1. Soak the black-eyed beans in water overnight. If using non-parboiled beans, first boil the beans for 10 minutes, then turn off the heat and allow them to soak in the hot water for 1 hour before draining.

2. Remove the skins. There are two methods to do this:

   METHOD 1: BY HAND

   Drain and wash the beans the next day. Rub the beans between your palms while they are submerged in water. The skins will float to the surface – skim them off and repeat until all skins have been removed.

   METHOD 2: USING A FOOD PROCESSOR

   Soak the beans in water for 10–15 minutes. Place a handful of beans and some water in a food processor or blender. Use the pulse setting to quickly start and stop the machine. (Pulse for no more than 3 seconds at a time.) This will help loosen the skins. Transfer the pulsed beans to a large bowl, cover with water and gently stir. The skins will float to the surface and you can skim them off. Repeat until all beans are peeled, then rinse the beans thoroughly. (Ensure that the skins are caught with a sieve so that you don't clog the drain.)

3. In a blender, combine the skinned beans, onion, garlic, Scotch bonnet peppers, red bell pepper and a small amount of water. Blend until smooth but thick in consistency.

4. Transfer the blended mixture to a bowl. Add the bouillon cube, coriander and salt to taste. Mix well.

5. Heat vegetable oil in a medium-sized frying pan over medium-high heat.

6. Scoop out 1 tbsp of the bean mixture per portion. Shape it into a patty with your hands, and carefully drop it into the hot oil.

7. Fry for 3 minutes on each side, until golden brown. Make sure you don't overcrowd the pan.

8. Drain the patties on paper towels.

9. Cut the buns in half and toast the cut sides of the buns in the same pan.

10. Assemble the burgers by layering the patties, lettuce, tomato slices and caramelised onions on the buns. Add a dollop of vegan mayonnaise and tomato sauce if desired.

FOOD IN AFRICA

THE GRAIN THAT REIGNS

As a child, I rarely attended weddings – my parents weren't big on having kids there. I only went to one, and that was because I was the flower girl. Something beautiful and fascinating happened that day; instead of cutting a Western cake, there was what we call in Kinyarwanda (one of the official languages of Rwanda) umutsima. This is sorghum pap or bread that is prepared specifically for weddings. And what's more, instead of cutting it using a knife, the couple used a thread.

I love the thought of having things that are authentically ours; things that don't lose their African authenticity, even if we improve them. I feel that sorghum is one of those grains that we can claim as being authentically African. This grain is not only gluten free, it's so versatile too. At that wedding, I was amused by the fact that the ordinary grain that mama used to make our soft porridge could turn into a celebration main dish at a wedding.

I would be lying if I said I have always appreciated indigenous foods. I only recently started to realise how much Africa has to offer and I have also discovered that the rest of the world wants what we have. On the other side of the coin, we often don't appreciate what we have. The other day I had an interesting conversation with my sister. I told her about my transition – how I've been shifting towards cooking and enjoying more indigenous African ingredients. I shared some of the recipes I have been making, for instance sorghum salads and replacing rice with sorghum. She was shocked that sorghum can be used in any way other than for simple soft porridge.

Later, I shared some ideas for a sorghum-based product with someone. She laughed and said it couldn't be done – unaware that I'd been testing it for a while. It not only worked, but was one of my best kitchen experiments.

Having these two conversations emphasised something that I always say: Africa's problems have nothing to do with having enough food, as this continent produces enough for us to eat. The real problem is that people don't know how to make the most of what grows here, how to distribute it equally and how to preserve it properly. While products like coffee or cocoa from Africa are exported all over the world, a large portion of locally grown food spoils after harvest – simply because there is often a lack of storage, transport or processing facilities.

Mafini Zamasaka

Sorghum Muffins

MAKES 12 MEDIUM OR 6 LARGE MUFFINS

- 1 tbsp flax meal
- 6 tbsp water
- 200 g (1 cup) granulated sugar
- 300 g (2½ cups) sorghum flour
- 70 g (½ cup) arrowroot flour
- 50 g (½ cup) cocoa powder
- 1 tsp baking powder
- 1 tsp bicarbonate of soda (baking soda)
- 100 g (½ cup) potato starch
- 1 tsp salt
- 150 ml (⅔ cup) soya milk (or any non-dairy milk)
- 150 ml (⅔ cup) grapeseed or other vegetable oil
- 1 tbsp apple cider vinegar
- 2 tsp vanilla extract
- 150 ml (⅔ cup) hot water

1. Preheat the oven to 180 °C (350 °F) and line a muffin pan with paper liners.

2. In a small bowl, mix the flax meal with the water to make "flax egg". Let it sit for 5–10 minutes to thicken.

3. In a large mixing bowl, whisk together the sugar, sorghum flour, arrowroot flour, cocoa powder, baking powder, bicarbonate of soda, potato starch and salt.

4. In another bowl, combine the prepared flax egg, soya milk, oil, apple cider vinegar and vanilla extract. Stir to mix well.

5. Slowly pour the wet mixture into the dry ingredients. Whisk everything together until well combined.

6. Carefully add the hot water and quickly whisk to ensure the batter stays smooth.

7. If the batter feels too thick, add a splash of soya milk or water (1–2 tbsp) to adjust the consistency.

8. Pour the batter into the lined muffin pan, filling each cup about ¾ full. Bake for 18–22 minutes or until a toothpick inserted into the centre of a muffin comes out clean.

9. Allow the muffins to cool in the pan for 10 minutes before transferring to a wire rack to cool completely.

WHAT IS SORGHUM?

Sorghum is an indigenous African grain that happens to be highly drought tolerant, which means it is an environmentally responsible crop, requires less water, grows well even in poor soils with minimal fertiliser and is naturally resistant to many pests and diseases, reducing the need for chemical pesticides. In addition to being a model sustainable crop, sorghum is high in dietary fibre and is also gluten free.

ETHIOPIA

SEVEN

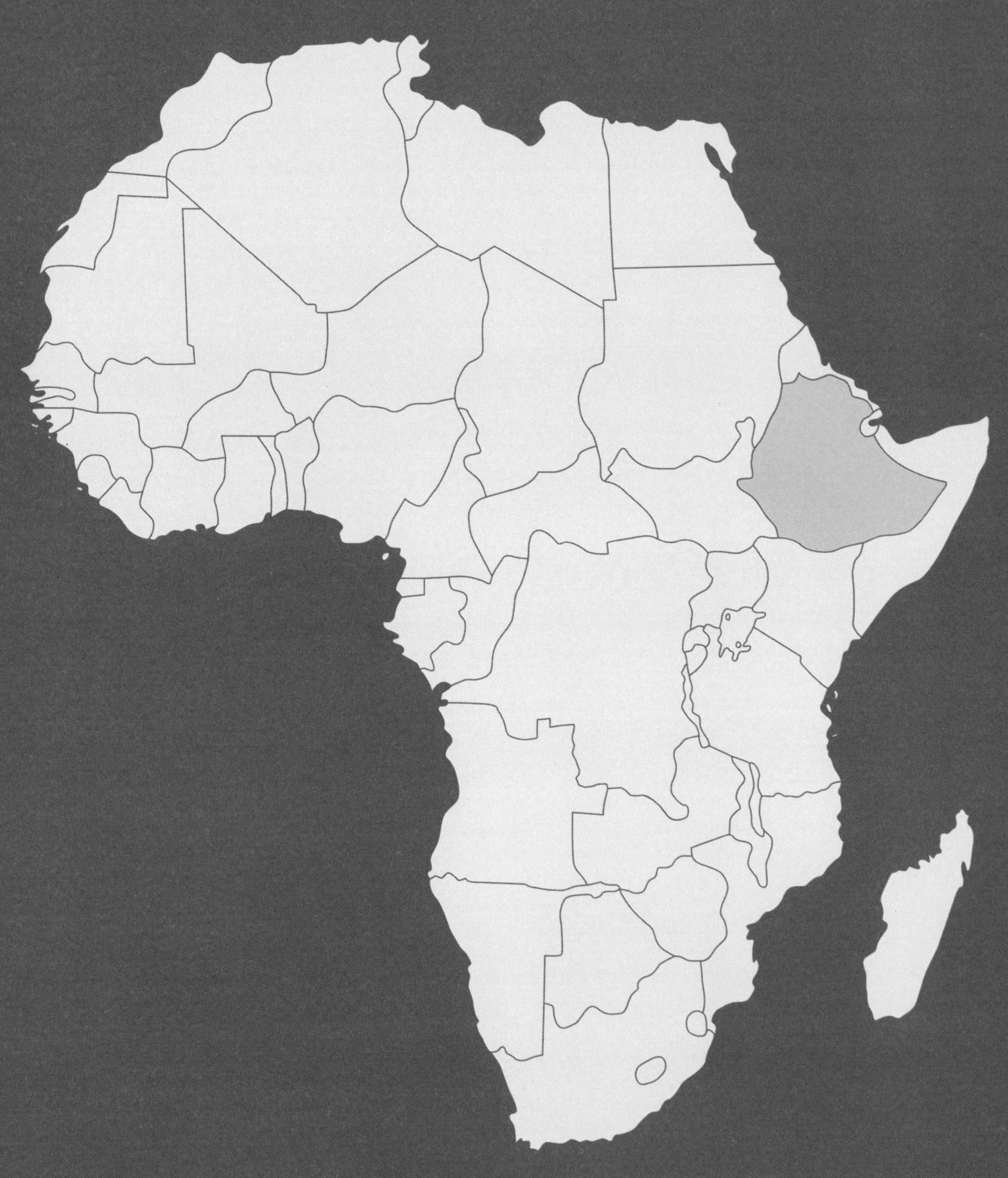

A COUNTRY WITH A COMMUNAL CUISINE

A country whose cuisine has been least diluted with outside influences is Ethiopia. Ethiopia has never been colonised, so I would like to believe that it might have fewer European influences engraved into its food culture.

Most vegans and vegetarians will tell you that Ethiopian cuisine is heaven for them. The variety of vegan and vegetarian food that accompanies a healthy sourdough bread made from an ancient African grain called teff is truly a reflection of how our forefathers lived. Another clear reflection of this is through sharing food and using it as a communion medium.

I was telling my friend Carmen how food is such a communal thing where I come from. As a child I learnt the significance and dynamics of community and sharing through how we approached food and mealtimes. Imagine finding yourself in a room with about 10 children and having to eat from the same plate with them every day!

My mother would place a large bamboo mat on the floor on which my siblings, cousins, friends and I could all fit. She would then dish our food onto one super large platter that we could all share from. This situation teaches you not to play with your food, otherwise at any time you could look up to find an empty platter.

During those mealtimes, we discovered the personalities of those who were seated on the mat with us. There was always that one person who had big hands and would grab big portions at every bite, without any consideration for those who were sharing the platter with them. Another person would gulp down their food, afraid that it might run out before they were full. There were those who watched others eat and then complained that they were finishing the food before they could get a chance to eat. Then there were those who would ask the youngest among us to leave them our last bites because they hadn't eaten as much as everyone else during the meal. It's amazing how these dynamics can be found in the people I meet in my everyday life, and I wonder which one of these people I am today.

When I visited an Ethiopian restaurant for the first time with my family, our meal was served on a large platter similar to the one my mother used when we were children. I remember those childhood memories flashing back and being reminded of the dynamics of life.

THANKSGIVING SEASONS

Through my upbringing, I have had the privilege of experiencing other African cultures through either people I have met along the way or countries and towns we lived in between Rwanda and South Africa. I have developed an overall understanding of different African cultures but sometimes I have felt that my understanding of Rwandan culture lacked depth. In recent years I have been intentional in not only developing a collective knowledge about different African cultures but also in really zooming in on Rwandan culture and food.

Just the other day, I kept seeing the word Umuganura in different Rwandan-based influencers' feeds. I then sent my sister Charlotte, who is based in Rwanda, a message asking what Umuganura was, and she took a long time to respond. It turns out that Umuganura is a public holiday in Rwanda, observed on the first Friday of August. This is Thanksgiving Day in Rwanda, and it's known as National Harvest Day – the celebration of the beginning of the harvest.

The meaning of the word Umuganura is the first-fruits festival. This festival can be traced back hundreds of years and is one of the most important ceremonies in the Rwandan culture. In days gone by, families would come together and dedicate their harvest to their ancestors for a blessing. We were a Christian family, and I remember that my mother would take the first fruits to church. I also remember communities coming together and bringing food to share in the celebration of Umuganura.

In modern days we harvest differently. Our harvests may not depend on farming, but we are all in pursuit of some kind of "harvest" or reward. It's a good thing to sometimes take time out from the act of pursuing to have Thanksgiving moments. Better yet, have them with a community around you, plus a table full of food.

In the spirit of Umuganura, where communities come together to share their harvests, the following recipes can be enjoyed as part of a Thanksgiving meal, whether served together on a platter or individually with injera.

Tikil Gomen

SERVES 5–6 AS A SIDE DISH

Ethiopian Cabbage

- 60 ml (¼ cup) olive oil (or less if preferred)
- 1 medium red onion, chopped
- 2 carrots, chopped
- 2 potatoes, chopped
- 1 tsp ground cumin
- 1 tsp ground black pepper
- 1 tsp ground ginger
- ½ tsp turmeric
- Salt to taste
- 180 g (6 oz) cabbage, chopped into big chunks

1. To a heated pan, add the oil and onion. Fry until the onion is translucent.
2. Add the carrots and potatoes.
3. Stir in the cumin, black pepper, ginger, turmeric and salt. Cover and cook for about 5 minutes or until the potatoes are soft.
4. Add the cabbage and mix well. Check seasoning and add more salt to taste.
5. Cover and cook for an additional 5 minutes or until all the vegetables are tender.

Kik Alicha

SERVES 5–6 AS A SIDE DISH

Ethiopian Split Pea Stew

- 150 g (5½ oz) yellow split peas
- 1 tbsp grapeseed or other vegetable oil
- 1 medium onion, chopped
- 5 garlic cloves, chopped
- 1 cm (½ inch) ginger, chopped
- ½ tsp ground turmeric
- ½ tsp ground black pepper
- Salt to taste
- 250 ml (1 cup) water
- 250 ml (1 cup) vegetable stock
- 1 tsp lemon juice

1. Soak the split peas in hot water for 30 minutes.
2. In a saucepan over medium heat, add the oil. Once hot, add the onion and sauté for 2 minutes until translucent.
3. Add the garlic and ginger, stirring to combine.
4. Stir in the turmeric, black pepper and salt. Mix well.
5. Drain the split peas and add them to the pot. Sauté until the peas are dry.
6. Pour in the water and vegetable stock. Cover and cook on medium-low heat for about 1 hour, stirring occasionally. Add the lemon juice and more water if needed.
7. Serve hot with injera.

Shiro Curry

SERVES 5–6 AS A SIDE DISH

Ethiopian-style Chickpea Curry

- 2 white onions, sliced
- 4 tbsp grapeseed or other vegetable oil
- 1 tbsp Ethiopian berbere spice (p. 152)
- ½ tsp cumin seeds (whole)
- 1 bay leaf
- 1 tomato, diced
- 1 tbsp tomato paste
- 300 g (10½ oz) cooked chickpeas (reserve some of the cooking liquid)
- Salt to taste
- 1 garlic clove, grated
- 1 tbsp vegan niter kibbeh (Ethiopian spiced clarified butter) (p. 155)
- Chopped coriander (cilantro), for garnish (optional)

1. In a large pot over medium heat, add the onions and allow them to sweat.
2. Add the oil, berbere spice, cumin and bay leaf. Cook for 5 minutes, stirring regularly.
3. Add the tomato and tomato paste. Mix well and cook for another 5–10 minutes.
4. Stir in the chickpeas with a little of the cooking liquid. Season with salt and let it simmer for a few more minutes.
5. Stir in the garlic and niter kibbeh. Mix well and garnish with coriander before serving.

Shiro Powder

MAKES
150 G (1½ CUPS)

- 125 g (1 cup) chickpea flour
- 1 tsp black cardamom
- 4 dried rue seeds (black seeds)
- ¼ tsp fenugreek seeds
- 1 tsp onion powder
- 3 tsp garlic powder
- 3 tsp sweet paprika
- 1 tsp chilli powder
- 1 tsp ground ginger
- ½ tsp turmeric
- Salt and pepper to taste

1. In a dry pan, roast the chickpea flour until slightly golden, being careful not to burn it. Transfer into a bowl.
2. Roast the whole spices (cardamom, rue seeds and fenugreek seeds) until fragrant, then grind them finely.
3. In a container, mix the chickpea flour, ground spices and remaining spices. Store in a dry container for future use. Add salt and pepper now or wait until later.

NOTE:

- If you have an Ethiopian grocery store nearby, you should be able to buy shiro powder.

Shiro Wat

SERVES 5–6 AS A SIDE DISH

Ethiopian Stew

- 1 onion (red or yellow), chopped
- 3–4 tbsp olive oil
- 1–2 tbsp berbere spice (use less if your heat tolerance is low) (p. 152)
- 1 tomato, diced
- 750 ml (3 cups) vegetable stock (or water)
- 60 g (½ cup) shiro powder (p. 148)
- 2–7 garlic cloves (3 recommended), minced
- Salt to taste
- Black pepper to taste
- 1 tbsp vegan niter kibbeh (Ethiopian spiced clarified butter) (p. 155)

1. In a large stockpot, cook the onions on medium-high heat for several minutes until they soften and become translucent. Stir frequently to prevent them from sticking.

2. Add the olive oil and cook for a few more minutes. Stir in 1–2 tbsp berbere spice, allowing it to cook for several minutes to develop flavour.

3. Stir in the tomato and cook for another 4–5 minutes.

4. Pour in half the vegetable stock and continue to simmer.

5. Gradually add the shiro powder, whisking to prevent clumping. Simmer for 15–20 minutes, adding more stock or water as needed to reach the desired thickness.

6. Stir in garlic, salt and pepper, simmering until bubbles appear (2–3 minutes). Finish by adding the niter kibbeh.

7. Serve with injera.

MY NEWFOUND LOVE OF LENTILS

The first time I ate lentils was in the refugee camp in the DRC. I didn't like them at all; I didn't like their smell or taste. Lentils were one of the things the United Nations Refugee Agency provided for the refugees in the camp. We had them in abundance, but we had no idea what to do with them. They really took some getting used to!

As I grew older, I learnt that lentils are so versatile and can absorb flavour well. I also learnt that they come in all sorts of shades, and red lentils have become one of my favourites. I make all kinds of curries with them and one of my favourites is misir wat (Ethiopian spiced red lentils). On average I make this delicious and spicy curry once a week.

Through this journey with lentils, I have learnt that just because your taste buds might be confused by an ingredient the first time you taste it doesn't mean you can't grow to love that same ingredient. Keep training your taste buds to appreciate things that your body needs. In the process, you will allow your ingredients to turn into whatever you like.

Misir Wat

SERVES 5–6 AS A SIDE DISH

Ethiopian Spiced Red Lentils

- 3 tbsp grapeseed or other vegetable oil
- 1 large yellow onion, very finely diced
- 3 garlic cloves, finely minced
- 1 Roma tomato, very finely chopped
- 3 tbsp tomato paste
- 1 tbsp berbere spice (less if your heat tolerance is low), (p. 152)
- 190 g (1 cup) red lentils, rinsed
- 250 ml (1 cup) vegetable broth
- 1 tsp salt
- 1 tbsp vegan niter kibbeh (Ethiopian spiced clarified butter, p. 155)

1. In a medium stockpot, heat the oil over medium-high heat. Add the onion and cook for 8–10 minutes until golden brown.
2. Stir in the garlic, tomato, tomato paste and 1 tbsp or less (as desired) of berbere spice. Cook for 5–7 minutes, stirring occasionally.
3. Add the lentils, vegetable broth and salt. Bring to a boil.
4. Reduce the heat to low, cover and simmer for about 30 minutes, stirring occasionally, until the lentils are soft. Add more broth if needed.
5. Stir in the niter kibbeh and simmer for a couple more minutes. Adjust salt to taste and serve with injera.

LOVE LANGUAGE

Regardless of what most people may think, I'm an introvert. I'm happiest when I'm alone in a quiet place. That's also when I'm most creative. Most of my friends will agree that I'm not one to show people love by spending time with them; as a matter of fact, I can go for years without seeing people in person, but it's not a reflection of how much I love them. What my family and friends can also attest to is that the first thing I will do to say "sorry" and "I love you" is to feed them. I take feeding people very seriously – my love language is food, and I spend half my income on feeding people!

When I'm not thinking about who to feed, I'm thinking about what to make; I also spend time learning to make all sorts of things, and I love being in the kitchen. Whereas other girls might collect beautiful outfits, you'll find me in a spice shop collecting spices I may never even use, simply because I have more than enough. However, one of the spice blends I'm always ready to use is berbere. I'm so obsessed with it that I often use it when I make a dish that is not Ethiopian. Even though berbere is the bedrock and essential part of Ethiopian cooking, it has become an essential part of my cooking, Ethiopian or not!

Berbere

MAKES 50 G (1 CUP)

Ethiopian Spice Blend

- 2 tsp coriander seeds
- 1 tsp cumin seeds
- ½ tsp fenugreek seeds
- ½ tsp black peppercorns
- ½ tsp whole allspice berries
- Seeds from 4 green cardamom pods
- 4 cloves
- 4–6 dried red chillies (seeds and membranes removed, broken into small pieces)
- 3 tbsp sweet paprika
- 1 tsp salt
- ¼ tsp nutmeg
- ½ tsp ground ginger
- ¼ tsp ground cinnamon
- 1 tsp ground turmeric

1. In a dry skillet over medium heat, add the coriander seeds, cumin seeds, fenugreek seeds, black peppercorns, allspice berries, cardamom seeds and cloves.
2. Toast the spices for about 3–5 minutes, stirring frequently, until they are very fragrant. Be careful not to scorch them, as this will make them bitter.
3. Once the whole spices are toasted, add the chillies to the skillet. Shake the pan regularly for an additional 1–2 minutes to toast the chillies slightly. Again, avoid scorching them.
4. Remove the skillet from the heat and transfer the toasted spice mixture to a bowl. Let it cool completely.
5. Once cooled, use a spice or coffee grinder to grind the mixture into a fine powder.
6. In a bowl, combine the ground spices with the remaining ingredients – sweet paprika, salt, nutmeg, ginger, cinnamon and turmeric. Grind everything together until well combined.
7. Transfer the spice blend to an airtight container and store it in a dark, cool place for up to 6 months.

NOTES:

- If you prefer a spicier blend, leave some of the seeds in the dried chillies.
- This blend can be used in a variety of dishes for added flavour and heat.

THE BATTLE FOR A "BETTER" BUTTER

Considering the bond we have created now, I feel that you deserve to know the amount of smell torture I went through in the name of beauty and clear skin. One Rwandan beauty tip is that the biggest secret to good skin is pure cow oil. Now that I think about it, this "cow oil" was basically unprocessed butter!

I remember being chased around the neighbourhood as a child because I refused to take an evening bath. Before you think that I hate bathing, it was never about the bath. It was about the sticky, smelly cow oil I was forced to rub into my skin. I didn't like the idea of smelling like rotten milk throughout the night, and eventually I think my mama got the message.

When I was exploring different African cuisines as an adult I met a lovely woman from Ethiopia, and she is responsible for my Ethiopian cooking skills, as I took cooking classes with her. As we were talking about food and Ethiopian ingredients, she told me that we had to buy Ethiopian clarified butter to add to every dish. I didn't like the idea, not because of my childhood butter trauma but because I'm following a plant-based lifestyle. I prefer using only plant-based ingredients, so I asked if we could do without the butter. She replied, "We definitely must have butter." She went on to explain that without the butter the food wasn't going to be the same.

I needed those cooking classes, so we had to reach a compromise. We had to develop a vegan version of the original clarified butter, and it turned out well! I can now safely say I have become a (vegan) butter person. The black cardamom we added to the "butter" and other spices gave it such a beautiful smell, which healed all my childhood butter traumas.

Vegan Niter Kibbeh

MAKES 200 G (1 CUP)

Ethiopian Spiced Clarified Butter

- 1 tsp whole black peppercorns
- 4 black (not green) cardamom pods
- 3 whole cloves
- 1 tsp fenugreek seeds
- 1 tsp coriander seeds
- 150 g (5½ oz) vegan butter
- 40 g (¼ cup) chopped yellow onion
- 1 tbsp minced garlic
- 1 tbsp minced ginger
- 1 cinnamon stick
- 1 tsp dried oregano
- 1 tsp cumin seeds
- 1 tsp ground nutmeg
- 1 tsp ground turmeric
- 1 tsp besobela (basil flowers)
- 1 tbsp kosseret (Lippia abyssinica, Ehtiopian verbena)

1. In a dry skillet over medium heat, add the peppercorns, cardamom pods, cloves, fenugreek seeds and coriander seeds.

2. Toast the spices for about 3–5 minutes, stirring frequently, until they are very fragrant. Be careful not to scorch them, as this will make them bitter. Set the toasted spices aside.

3. In a medium saucepan, combine the butter, onion, garlic, ginger, toasted spices, cinnamon stick, oregano, cumin seeds, nutmeg, turmeric, besobela and kosseret.

4. Bring the mixture to an extremely low simmer. Continue to simmer over low heat for 1–1.5 hours. Be very careful not to burn the butter, as burnt butter will taste bitter and cannot be salvaged.

5. After simmering, pour everything through a fine-mesh cheesecloth or strainer into a jar. There's no need to skim off the foam, as everything will be removed during straining.

6. Allow the niter kibbeh to cool completely. Seal the jar to ensure it is airtight.

NOTE:

- It will keep at room temperature for several weeks, in the fridge for at least a couple of months and even longer in the freezer. (It will be hard in the fridge and freezer, so let it come to room temperature to make it easier to scoop it.)

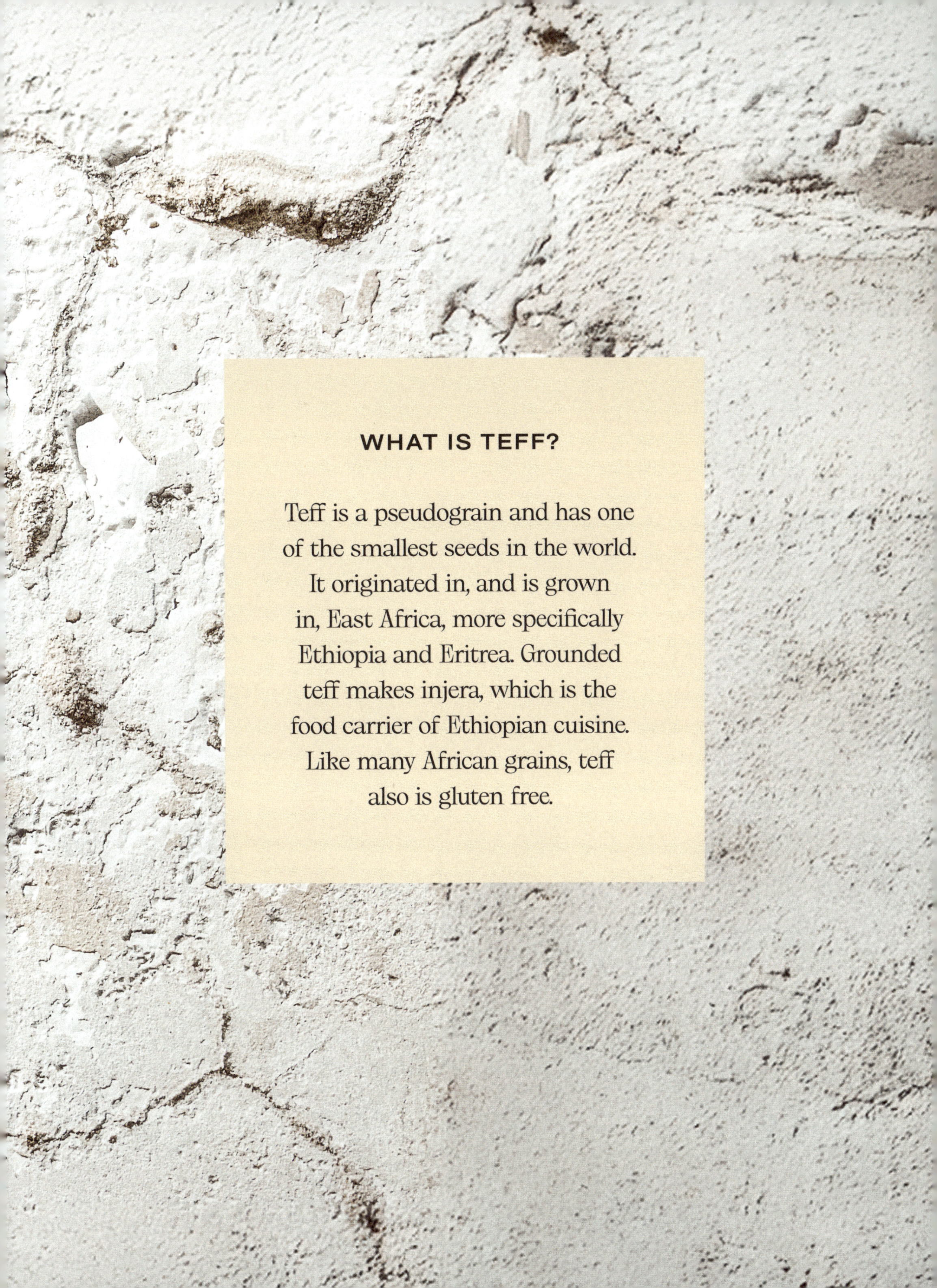

WHAT IS TEFF?

Teff is a pseudograin and has one of the smallest seeds in the world. It originated in, and is grown in, East Africa, more specifically Ethiopia and Eritrea. Grounded teff makes injera, which is the food carrier of Ethiopian cuisine. Like many African grains, teff also is gluten free.

NIGERIA

EIGHT

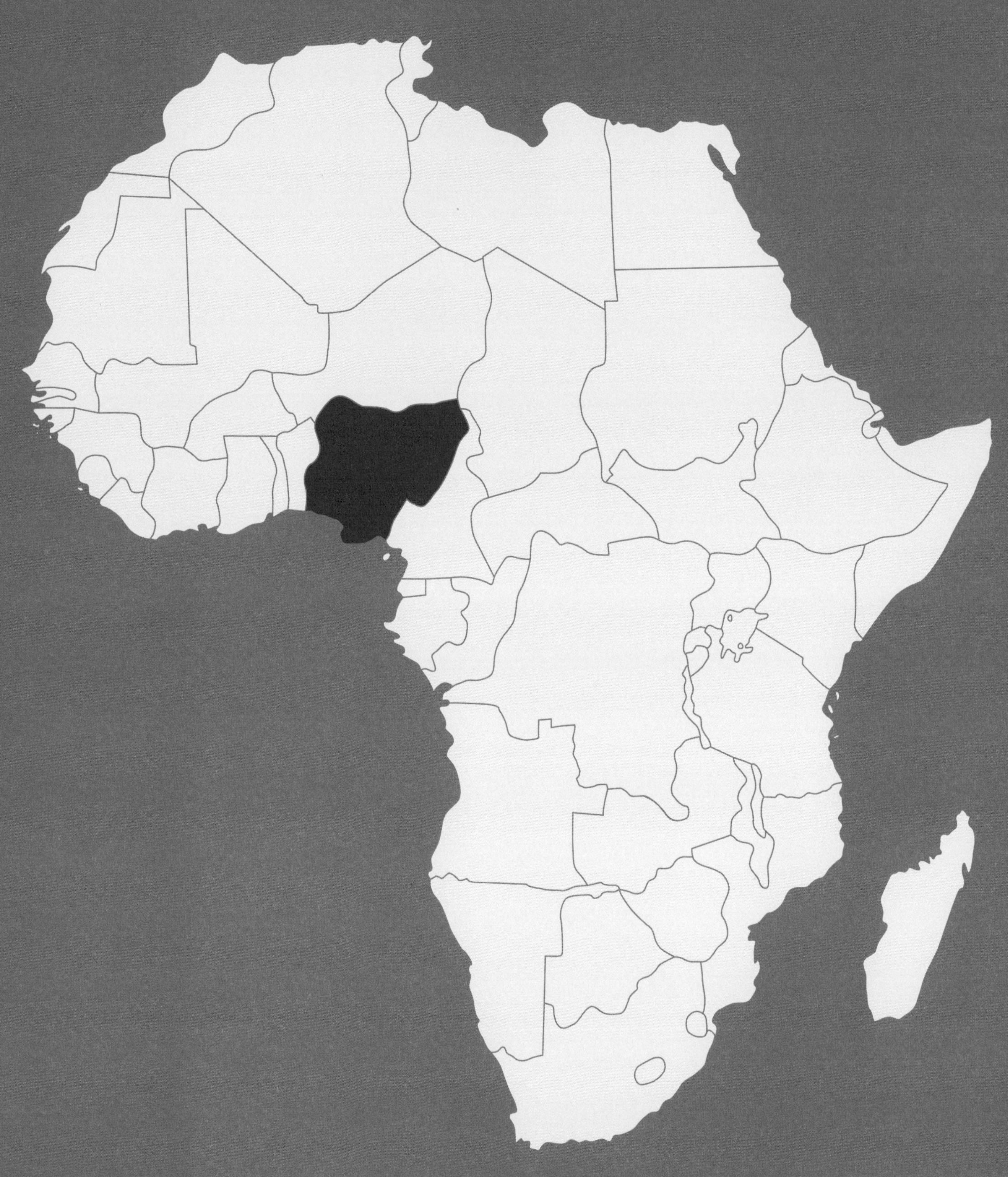

WHEN EATING GARI, RIGHT IS RIGHT

It's true that throughout Africa we have certain things that set us apart, such as languages, but one thing for sure is that we have the same world view. When I was a little girl, my dad took my brother and me to eat in a restaurant during our time in Uganda on our way to Kenya. From the time our food was served until we finished our meals, everyone in the restaurant kept staring at me.

Some of the guests in that restaurant would look at me and then start talking, and they made it clear that I was at the centre of the conversation. This continued, and their staring made me extremely uncomfortable. Finally, one man was courageous enough to come to our table. He asked my dad if it was possible for him to ask me to stop using my left hand when eating my food.

I once had an interesting conversation about this issue with a friend from Nigeria, who told me that Nigerians have similar beliefs. It turns out that culturally, the left hand is considered dirty and is only reserved for bathroom activities. Eating and greeting people using this hand is considered disrespectful and ill-mannered. To be safe, when eating a meal with your hands in Africa (and many meals are eaten with the hands on this continent), use your right hand, including when digging into gari.

Gari

SERVES 1

Fermented Starchy Cassava Ball

250 ml (1 cup) water

40 g (1/3 cup) gari (adjust as needed for texture)

1. In a saucepan, bring the water to a boil.
2. Remove the saucepan from the heat. Gradually stir in the gari using a wooden spatula or spoon. Mix well to combine.
3. If the mixture is too soft for your liking, continue to add more gari, a little at a time, until you achieve the desired consistency. Stir thoroughly after each addition.
4. Once the desired texture is reached, mould the gari into your preferred shape and serve immediately, ideally alongside egusi soup.

NOTE:

- Gari is versatile, so feel free to adjust the amount used based on your texture preference.

GOING BACK TO MY FOOD ROOTS

For the longest time, I used seasoning cubes like everyone else. It's what we knew. They were convenient and tasty, and could always be found in the kitchen drawer. I never really stopped to ask what was in them or where the flavours came from. But as I started diving deeper into African food and trying to reconnect with where I come from, I kept coming across this word: dawadawa.

West Africans – especially Ghanaians – spoke about it with so much pride. Some remembered it from their grandmothers' kitchens, others from the street food back home. I got curious. I really wanted to try it.

I found out that dawadawa comes from the African locust bean tree. The seeds are fermented and used to season food. And honestly, when I opened my first little packet, I wasn't sure what to expect. The smell was strong and earthy – so different from the commercial stuff I was used to. But there was something about it that felt ... real.

Then I had this moment of realisation: I've probably walked past those trees before, maybe even stepped over the pods on the ground, without knowing they held food inside. All that time, I was surrounded by something deeply connected to who I am and where I come from, and I didn't even notice. That hit me.

I used to think food was just about flavour. Now I see it's also about memory, culture and identity. Cooking with dawadawa feels like letting my ancestors into the kitchen. It's grounding, humbling – and honestly, it tastes amazing. These days, I always use dawadawa instead of conventional stock cubes, and I try to look around me more. I want to know the names of the trees. I want to ask the old ladies at the market how they cook. I want to remember. Because food is more than what's on the plate. It's a way of coming home.

Egusi Soup

SERVES 4

Melon Seeds Soup

- 290 g (2 cups) egusi seeds
- 60 g (1/4 cup) African red palm oil
- 1 onion
- 1 Scotch bonnet pepper, seeds removed
- 1 red bell pepper, roughly diced
- 185–250 ml (3/4–1 cup) water, plus extra as needed
- 250 ml (1 cup) vegetable stock
- Soya sauce (for additional flavour, optional)
- 10 g (1/3 oz) dawadawa seeds (locust beans, about 2 pinches)
- 1 medium eggplant (aubergine), diced
- 1/2 punnet (about 200 g/2 cups) white mushrooms, sliced
- Soya strips (optional, or substitute with oyster mushrooms)

1. Make sure there are no stones in the egusi seeds and wipe them using a clean cloth or paper towels. Blend the seeds in a blender or food processor until you achieve a fine paste. You can add a little water if necessary to help blend them.

2. In a large pot, heat the oil over medium heat. Once the oil is hot, add the blended egusi paste to the pot. Fry the egusi, stirring continuously, for about 5–7 minutes until it starts to turn golden and fragrant.

3. In a blender, combine the onion, Scotch bonnet pepper and red bell pepper. Blend until smooth.

4. Add the blended vegetable mixture to the fried egusi. Stir well to combine.

5. Gradually add 185–250 ml water, stirring continuously. Cook over medium or medium-low heat until the mixture begins to thicken and you hear a spluttering sound, indicating it is drying out (about 10–15 minutes). It should resemble scrambled eggs.

6. Pour in the vegetable stock and add the soya sauce (if using). Stir to mix. Add the locust beans and stir to combine. Then add the eggplant, mushrooms and soya strips (if using).

7. Allow the soup to cook for an additional 5–10 minutes until the vegetables are tender and everything is well incorporated. Stir occasionally.

8. Remove from heat and serve hot, ideally with fufu or rice.

NOTES:

- The locust beans add a unique umami flavour, similar to fish sauce, but their smell mellows as they cook.
- Substitute the mushrooms with different types of your choice (I used oyster and button mushrooms).

WEST AFRICAN FAVOURITES

Nigerians are possibly the most confident people in Africa. They walk with confidence in a way that puts the rest of Africa to shame.

They have managed to get us to buy into not only their movies but also their food. It's amazing what self-love can accomplish. For example, if there is anyone around who doesn't know what jollof rice is, then that person has been living under a rock and needs intervention.

I mention jollof because it's such a brilliant example of how well Nigerians have marketed their cuisine. For the longest time, I resisted the forces that were pushing me towards the jollof trend in my attempt to remain proudly East African because I believed pilau rice needed more shine than jollof. I really tried. I'm still trying even now, but let's give credit where it's due! Nigerians have done more in setting the stage for African foods than the rest of the continent has. As someone who is an advocate for revolutionising African food, I respect them for it.

Some time back, I made a spread of different African foods, mainly East African cuisine. As I was explaining the dishes, I mentioned that we (East Africans) also have our own jollof. I saw the excitement on my guests' faces, as they had never tasted jollof but had only heard of it. They couldn't wait to taste East Africa's jollof. I realised then that as Africans, marketing our foods is the first step to placing our souls on the world map. This is to increase the world's appetite to not only search for our foods but also to connect with us on an emotional level through African cuisine.

If making jollof rice will put a smile on people's faces and connect them to Africa through food, then I'm all in. Count on me to make not only jollof but as many other West African dishes as I can think of.

Lately, my favourite West African food has been moi moi. I love the way it melts in your mouth, as though you are eating something other than steamed beans.

Moi Moi

SERVES 6

Steamed Bean Pudding

- 300 g (10½ oz) dried black-eyed beans
- 2 large red bell peppers, seeds removed
- 1 large onion, chopped
- 1–2 Scotch bonnet peppers (adjust to taste)
- 4 garlic cloves, pressed
- 2 vegetable stock cubes
- 2½ tsp salt
- 1 tsp smoked paprika
- 75 ml (5 tbsp) grapeseed or other vegetable oil
- A handful of fresh coriander (cilantro) and red onions, minced

THE NIGHT BEFORE

1. Rinse the black-eyed beans and remove any dirt. Place them in a large bowl and cover with hot water, ensuring it is at least 5 cm (2 inches) above the beans. Let them soak for at least 1 hour.
2. Drain the water from the beans and transfer them to a food processor. Blitz for about 10 pulses to break them up slightly.
3. Return the beans to the bowl, cover with hot water and agitate. The skins will float to the top.
4. Use a slotted spoon to skim off the floating skins and dispose of them. Stir the beans with your hands, rubbing them together to release more skins, and repeat the skimming process until most of the skins have been removed.
5. Once done, cover the beans with hot water and soak them overnight.

To avoid the above steps, you can use red lentils instead and soak them for at least an hour. After soaking, rinse the red lentils and proceed with blending them (step 3 below).

THE NEXT DAY

1. Preheat the oven to 180 °C (350 °F). Spray your tins or oven-safe moulds such as ramekins with cooking spray and set them aside.
2. In the food processor, combine the red bell peppers, onion, Scotch bonnet peppers, garlic cloves and stock cubes. Process until smooth.
3. Blend the black-eyed beans or red lentils: drain the black-eyed beans or lentils and add them to the food processor or blender. Process until you have a smooth mixture. If needed, add a small amount of water to help blend, but avoid making it too watery. The goal is a creamy consistency.
4. Once smooth, add the salt, smoked paprika and oil. Blitz again until well incorporated.

5. Transfer the mixture to a bowl and stir in the coriander.

6. Fill a large baking tin halfway with hot water. This will create a water bath for the moulds.

7. Fill your prepared moulds with the moi moi mixture, filling them about halfway. Cover each mould tightly with tinfoil.

8. Carefully transfer the moulds to the oven and bake for 2–2½ hours. The moi moi is done when the sides start to pull away from the moulds.

9. Once cooked, allow the moi moi to cool slightly before either serving them in the moulds or inverting them onto a plate.

NOTE:

- Adjust the number of Scotch bonnet peppers based on your heat preference.

THE BEST OF BOTH WORLDS

I'm a late bloomer. When my peers had already developed curvy chests, had boyfriends and were messing up, I was busy trying to figure out my place in this world. We never really stayed in one place long enough for me to find my space, and feeling displaced made me stand out. In some places, it was because of how I spoke or how I was not able to speak at all. In other places it was because of my dark skin, or simply because as a foreigner I just looked different. I desperately wanted to fit in, but I knew it was impossible.

At our church potlucks I would look at all the amazing dishes people had made. I thought that I would never be able to take my food to church because it didn't look good enough. When I started making money and was able to afford to buy food, I always looked up Western recipes to make so that I could also impress people around me. I thought my traditional food wasn't good enough, and I tried so hard to find my place in this world by running away from who I really was. Being part of a diaspora community made things worse, as I was too foreign for the places I lived in, but I was also too diluted for home.

As I was looking for a dish to represent my current space in the world, I thought of this rich tomato sauce and plantain dumplings recipe. I feel that it's the best of both worlds – a theme that I have learnt to accept and love. I have been given the privilege to live a colourful life influenced by every place I have been to and everyone I have met, and yet I remain authentically and unapologetically African. For someone who has never found a proper settlement, I have managed to find a solid space for Africa in my heart.

NOTES:

- Adjust the amount of salt and herbs according to your taste preference.
- Feel free to add other vegetables to the stew for added flavour and nutrition.

Plantain Dumplings in Coconut Tomato Stew

SERVES 5

- 1 tbsp grapeseed or other vegetable oil
- 1 onion, diced
- 3 garlic cloves, minced
- ½ tsp dried thyme
- 1 tsp turmeric
- 2 large tomatoes, diced
- Salt to taste
- 200 ml (scant 1 cup) coconut milk
- 1 vegan bouillon cube
- 410 ml (1⅔ cups) water, divided

For the dumplings

- 2 large plantains, not fully ripe
- 250 g (2 cups) bread flour
- ½ tsp salt
- 1 red bell pepper, diced
- Handful of fresh basil or parsley, chopped

1. In a saucepan, heat the oil over medium heat. Once heated, add the onion and sauté until translucent (about 3–4 minutes). Add the garlic, thyme and turmeric, and sauté for an additional 1 minute.
2. Stir in the tomatoes and season with salt. Cook for about 5 minutes until the tomatoes soften.
3. Pour in the coconut milk and add the bouillon cube. Bring the mixture to a simmer and cook for about 3 minutes.
4. Add 100 ml (a scant ½ cup) water and bring the pot to a boil. Then reduce the heat to a simmer while you prepare the dumplings.
5. Peel the plantains. Using a box grater, grate them using the smallest holes. Place the grated plantain in a bowl.
6. Add the bread flour and salt. Mix to combine.
7. Gradually add the rest of the water, a little at a time, kneading the mixture to form a dough ball. If the dough is too sticky, add extra flour. If it's too dry, add a little more water.
8. Divide the dough into 9–10 equal parts. Roll each piece into a smooth ball with your hands.
9. Add the red bell pepper and half the chopped basil to the stew pot and stir them in.
10. Neatly place the dumplings on top of the simmering stew, ensuring there is enough liquid to cook them without completely submerging them. If necessary, add a bit more water to the pot.
11. Cover the pot and cook the dumplings for 30–40 minutes over low to medium heat, ensuring they are steaming in the stew.
12. Once cooked, garnish with the remaining fresh basil before serving them alongside the flavourful stew

THE SIMPLE THINGS IN LIFE

Unfortunately, when I was growing up I, like many children, didn't appreciate healthy meals. As I mentioned earlier, I was sickly as a child and my mama wanted to make sure that I ate healthily. She often had to bribe me to get me to drink my sorghum porridge, and one way she did this was to give me sweet potatoes with my porridge for breakfast.

I loved the sweetness and creaminess of the sweet potatoes in Rwanda. I used to think that all sweet potatoes tasted the same until I left Rwanda, when I discovered that they are not all created equal. Needless to say, South African sweet potatoes don't taste like the ones in Rwanda. So, I decided to find a replacement for the taste of my childhood – and I found it in plantain chips.

I have learnt that the simple things in life add more value, and I have since developed a respect for them. Three simple ingredients come together in this dish to create a West African comfort treat that's become one of my favourites.

Fried plantain has taught me that food doesn't have to be complicated and intimidating. Sometimes, the simpler the better. The only downside to fried plantain is that you will be left wanting more, no matter how much you have had.

Fried Plantains

SERVES 2–3

- 2 ripe plantains, sliced
- Salt (optional, to taste)
- 250 ml (1 cup) oil for frying (e.g. sunflower oil)

1. Peel the plantains. Slice them diagonally into thick slices (about 1 cm/½ inch thick) and place them in a bowl.
2. If using salt, sprinkle it over the plantains and toss to coat evenly.
3. Add the oil to a frying pan. Heat it over medium heat until it is hot. (Test the heat by dropping a small piece of plantain into the oil – it should sizzle immediately.)
4. Carefully arrange the plantains in the hot oil, spacing them to prevent sticking.
5. Fry the plantains on medium heat for about 5 minutes or until they turn golden brown. Because of the natural sugars in plantains, they can burn quickly, so keep a close eye on them.
6. Once they are golden brown on one side, use tongs or a spatula to turn them over and fry the other side until golden brown as well.
7. Once both sides are cooked, transfer the fried plantains to a plate lined with paper towel to drain the excess oil.
8. Serve the fried plantains warm.

NOTES:

- Adjust the thickness of the slices based on your preference for texture. Thicker slices will be softer and thinner slices will be crispier.
- Feel free to serve the plantains with a dipping sauce.
- They can also be enjoyed as a side dish.

FOOD IN AFRICA

THE PALM OIL PREDICAMENT

At some point we have to deal with the elephant in the room: palm oil. The truth is, it's difficult to avoid it, and it's one of the most versatile food products in the world. Chances are you have seen it in most of the ingredients used to produce your favourite processed foods. It's also possibly one of the most controversial ingredients after meat and dairy.

For so long I didn't understand how this ingredient, which was used in my mother's kitchen for years to prepare food, has been labelled a danger not only to the environment but also to our health. I started doing my own research to settle the uneasy feeling in my gut. One of the most dangerous things to do is to take anything at face value, without taking time to engage with a particular issue and understand it. Not only did I discover that all palm oils are not created equal, but I also found out that African palm fruit oil can actually be good for us.

Whenever we address palm oil issues, we should always know which type of palm oil we are referring to. Let's start with unrefined red palm oil that is pressed from the fruit of the red palm. Some scientists have named it a superfood because of its medicinal use.

We then have the most used palm oil, which is light yellow in colour and is highly refined. Palm growth has expanded to Southeast Asia, including Malaysia and Indonesia. These two countries currently produce more than 80% of the world's palm oil supply. So, much of the palm oil on the market is from Southeast Asia, where there has been widespread destruction of rainforests, resulting in habitat loss for key species such as orangutans. This has in turn increased the release of gases that contribute to climate change and seizure of land owned by indigenous people.

All in all, whenever sourcing palm oil, always look for red palm oil that is sourced from Africa and certified sustainable. In fact, red palm oil has been used for medicinal purposes throughout Africa for many years because of its health benefits. Red palm oil is less refined than bleached palm oil. The refinement process involved in producing red palm oil removes fewer nutrients, which makes red palm oil a potentially healthier alternative to standard palm oil.

A SUSTAINABLE AFRICAN STAPLE

Keeping in mind the benefits of unrefined red palm oil, let's dive into a recipe that celebrates this sustainable and nutritious ingredient. This dish not only incorporates the unique flavour of red palm oil but also connects us with traditional African culinary practices.

Ensure that the palm oil you use is unrefined and sourced sustainably from Africa. This ingredient will enhance the dish while supporting both your health and the environment.

Cassava Root with African Red Palm Oil

SERVES 4

- 1 cassava root (about 25 cm/10 inches)
- A pinch of salt
- 1 tsp onion powder
- 1 tsp garlic powder
- 1 tsp chilli flakes (adjust based on spice preference)
- 1 tsp cumin
- 1 tsp ground black pepper
- 4 tbsp African red palm oil
- Handful of chopped spring onions (scallions; optional, for garnish)
- Handful of minced coriander (cilantro), for garnish

1. Cut off the ends of the cassava root. Peel off all the waxy brown skin, ensuring only the white part remains.

2. Cut the white root into bite-sized sticks (approximately 2½–5 cm/1–2 inches long).

3. In a saucepan, bring water to a boil over medium heat. Add a pinch of salt and the cassava to the boiling water.

4. Boil until the cassava softens and begins to turn translucent (about 35 minutes).

5. In a small bowl, mix the onion powder, garlic powder, chilli flakes, cumin and black pepper. Preheat the oven to 180 °C (350 °F).

6. Once the cassava is cooked, remove it from the pot and drain well. Place the cooked cassava in a large bowl and generously sprinkle with the spice mixture. Drizzle the red palm oil over the cassava and toss to coat evenly.

7. Spread out the seasoned cassava pieces on a parchment-lined baking sheet. Bake for 20 minutes. Halfway through baking, turn the pieces over to ensure they don't dry out.

8. Once baked, remove from the oven and garnish with the spring onions and coriander.

9. Serve hot.

NOTES:

- Ensure the cassava is cooked through and tender before coating and baking.
- Adjust the spice amounts according to your flavour preference.
- This dish pairs well with a variety of dips or sauces for added flavour.

WHAT IS AFRICAN RED PALM OIL?

This particular palm oil is high in vitamins A and E. The oil's deep red-orange colour is the giveaway that it is not palm kernel oil but is from the fruit itself. The colour also reveals the oil's antioxidant content in the form of beta-carotene, as well as rare tocotrienols and tocopherols from the vitamin E family.

GHANA

NINE

COCOA HEAVEN

I recently learnt that Ghana and Côte d'Ivoire are practically the world-leading forces in the production and exportation of the cocoa beans that most countries use to produce our beloved chocolates. As a child I didn't make the link between chocolate and Africa. I remember my friends and I harassing anyone we assumed was from Europe or America, or had visited there, asking them to give us chocolates. We believed that these people were the closest we would ever get to chocolates, and what's more, most people literally fed our stereotype – whoever came back home from Europe or America brought chocolates as gifts.

Côte d'Ivoire is the leading producer of cocoa beans, as well as cashew nuts, in the world, but it is not the main manufacturer of either chocolate or cashew nut products. That, right there, is another problem Africans have. We lack the knowledge of food preservation and food processing, which would significantly alleviate hunger and poverty across the continent.

Chocolate Pudding

SERVES 5

For the bottom cake layer
100 g (½ cup) granulated sugar
150 g (⅛ cup) cake flour
1 tsp salt
35 g (⅔ cup) cocoa powder
2 tsp baking powder
70 g (2½ oz) coconut oil
125 ml (½ cup) plant-based milk
2 tsp vanilla extract

For the middle powder layer
70 g (⅓ cup) granulated sugar
70 g (⅓ cup) brown sugar
½ tsp salt
35 g (⅔ cup) cocoa powder

For the top water layer
125 ml (½ cup) hot water

1. Preheat the oven to 180 °C (350 °F).
2. Lightly grease individual baking tins or foil moulds and place them on a baking sheet.

THE BOTTOM CAKE LAYER

1. To a large bowl, add the sugar, flour, salt, cocoa powder and baking powder. Mix until well combined.
2. Melt the coconut oil and add it to the dry ingredients along with the plant-based milk and vanilla extract. Stir until just combined; do not overmix.
3. Pour the batter into the prepared individual baking dishes, filling them to less than halfway to leave enough room for the second layer and water. Use a spoon to spread the mixture evenly across the dishes.

THE MIDDLE POWDER LAYER

1. In a separate bowl, mix the granulated sugar, brown sugar, salt and cocoa powder.
2. Sprinkle the powder mixture evenly over the bottom cake layer in each mould. Start with a spoonful and add more as needed.

THE TOP WATER LAYER

1. Carefully pour the hot water on top of the powder layer in each mould, a little at a time. Avoid overfilling and do not mix; it should look like a puddle on top.
2. Bake for 15–25 minutes, or until a knife or cake tester inserted into the centre comes out clean, with no wet batter clinging to it.
3. Let the chocolate pudding cool for about 15 minutes before serving. Serve warm.

NOTES:

- To keep the texture light, make sure you don't overmix the batter.
- Adjust the baking time based on the oven; the pudding should be slightly soft in the centre when done.
- This pudding pairs wonderfully with non-dairy ice cream and raspberries.

Vegan White Chocolate Ice Cream Sundae

SERVES 4

For the ice cream

- 400 ml (1⅔ cups) full-fat coconut milk
- 100 ml (scant ½ cup) vegan cream (such as Orley Whip or any plant-based cream)
- 70 g (⅓ cup) granulated sugar
- ¼ tsp salt
- 2 tbsp cornflour (cornstarch)
- 2 tbsp water
- 50 g (1¾ oz) cocoa butter
- 1½ tsp vanilla extract
- 1 tsp xanthan gum (optional)

For the strawberry compote

- 200 g (7 oz) strawberries, hulled and halved, plus extra for garnish
- 20 g (¾ oz) caster sugar (superfine sugar)
- 1 tbsp icing sugar (confectioners' sugar)
- Juice and zest of ½ lemon
- 1 tsp arrowroot powder or cornflour (cornstarch)
- 3 tbsp water
- Mint leaves (optional, for garnish)

ICE CREAM PREPARATION

1. Place the ice cream machine bowl in the freezer at least 24 hours in advance, ensuring it's frozen solid, with no liquid sloshing when shaken.

2. In a saucepan, combine the coconut milk, cream, sugar and salt.

3. In a small bowl, whisk the cornflour with the water to make a slurry. Add this slurry to the saucepan, along with the cocoa butter.

4. Heat over medium heat, stirring occasionally, until the mixture thickens and coats the back of a spoon (about 6–8 minutes). Do not let it boil.

5. Remove from heat and stir in the vanilla extract and xanthan gum (if using).

6. Pour the ice cream base into a shallow container. Let it cool to room temperature on a counter.

7. Cover the surface with cling film and refrigerate for at least 4 hours or overnight.

8. Once chilled, pour the mixture into the ice cream machine and churn until it reaches a soft-serve consistency (10–20 minutes, depending on your machine).

9. Transfer the ice cream to a freezer-safe container. Press parchment paper or wax paper against the surface to prevent ice crystals forming. Seal the container and freeze for at least 4 hours to harden.

STRAWBERRY COMPOTE PREPARATION

1. In a saucepan, combine the strawberries, caster sugar, icing sugar, lemon zest and lemon juice. Cook over medium heat until the strawberries soften slightly and the sugar dissolves.

2. Set aside half the strawberries and some of the juice for later use.

3. In a small bowl, mix the arrowroot powder with the water. Stir this mixture into the remaining strawberries in the saucepan.

4. Cook while stirring continuously until the sauce thickens. If it becomes too thick, add a little more water. Once thickened, remove from heat and allow it to cool completely.

5. In serving glasses, start with a spoonful of the strawberry compote.

6. Add a scoop of the ice cream, followed by another layer of compote.

7. Add another scoop of ice cream and drizzle with the reserved strawberry sauce.

8. Garnish with fresh strawberries and mint leaves.

FRIENDLY FOOD RIVALRY

Throughout the 21st century, Africa as a continent has been through so many conflicts. Africans have lost their loved ones, homes and livelihoods because of these ongoing wars. However, there is one peaceful "war" that continues to rage in Africa and frankly, we don't want this war to end. Jollof rice wars between West African countries have been a great sign of pride and heritage.

Though jollof has its origin in Senegal, both Ghana and Nigeria have placed it on the world map. You can always be sure to have a healthy and funny debate whenever jollof is involved. One of my favourite stories is of a Nigerian man who was asked who, between Ghana and Nigeria, makes better jollof. He responded by saying: "The best jollof I ate was in Ghana made by a Nigerian chef." Talk about someone who knows how to cover his bases!

A jollof feud is a sign of passion. It keeps countries on their toes to keep improving their dish and it keeps chefs accountable to represent the dish with dignity and originality. As a chef, one thing is for sure: you don't want to end up on the wrong side of a jollof war.

Jollof Rice

SERVES 6–8

- 2 large tomatoes
- 2 medium red bell peppers
- 2 Scotch bonnet peppers (remove seeds for less heat)
- 2 medium yellow onions, chopped
- 4 garlic cloves, minced
- 2 tsp fresh ginger, grated
- 80 ml (1/3 cup) grapeseed or other vegetable oil
- 2 tbsp tomato paste
- 2 bay leaves
- Salt to taste
- 2 tsp dried thyme
- 1½ tsp curry powder
- 4 cardamom pods
- 1 tsp smoked paprika
- 630 g (3 cups) long-grain basmati rice, uncooked and rinsed
- 1 litre (4 cups) reduced-sodium vegetable broth
- Fresh herbs of your choice, for garnish

1. In a blender, combine the tomatoes, red bell peppers, Scotch bonnet peppers, half the chopped onions, half the garlic and 1 tsp ginger. Blend until smooth.

2. Heat the oil in a large pot over medium heat. Add the rest of the chopped onions and sauté for about 3 minutes until softened.

3. Add the tomato paste to the pot and cook for about 2 minutes, stirring occasionally.

4. Stir in the remaining garlic and ginger. Cook for another 2 minutes, stirring frequently.

5. Pour in the blended pepper and tomato puree. Add the bay leaves and simmer for 10–12 minutes, stirring occasionally, until the sauce thickens.

6. Stir in the salt, thyme, curry powder, cardamom pods and smoked paprika. Let the mixture cook for an additional 2 minutes.

7. Stir the rice into the sauce, making sure it's fully coated. Add the vegetable broth and stir to combine.

8. Bring the mixture to a boil, then cover the pot with tinfoil and a lid to trap the steam. Reduce the heat to low and cook for 30–40 minutes or until the rice is fully cooked and has absorbed all the liquid.

9. Fluff the rice with a fork, remove the bay leaves and cardamom pods, and garnish with fresh herbs of your choice. Top the rice with fried plantains (p. 171), if desired.

FULL OF BEANS – AND LOVIN' IT

When I was growing up, the definition of being broke in our home was having no beans in our pantry. That meant things were really rough! We ate so many beans when I was a child that I promised myself that when I grew up and had a home of my own, there would be no signs of beans in it. Well, let's just say that old habits die hard, and some promises are meant to be broken. My home is a paradise for lovers of beans! I eat them at least once a week and run to the grocery store the minute I realise I'm out of them.

I'm not sure if I should blame my upbringing for my newfound love of beans or if I should just admit that beans are delicious and that every pantry should have them. While having a conversation with my friend Esi from Ghana, she mentioned that she had a similar bean experience when she was growing up, but that she still can't shake the bean memory. So, since beans will always be part of our lives, we decided to start exchanging recipes and talk about our positive memories of beans.

She introduced me to a dish called "red red", which is black-eyed beans cooked in palm oil. She described it with so much excitement and in such detail that my mouth started watering, and I knew I would have to add something similar to my world of food. My friend isn't someone who writes out recipes, so she gave me an idea of what was needed and I had to figure out how to bring it together in a language I could understand. It was so delicious and it inspired me to renew my commitment to my relationship with beans.

Red Red Beans

SERVES 4

- 400 g (14 oz) dried black-eyed beans (cowpeas)
- 80 g (3 oz) African red palm oil
- 1 medium red onion, chopped
- 1 tsp minced ginger
- 1 Scotch bonnet pepper, finely chopped (remove seeds for less heat)
- ½ tsp cayenne pepper (optional, adjust for spice level)
- 1 tsp curry powder
- 1 tsp smoked paprika
- 6 plum tomatoes, chopped
- 80 g (3 oz) tomato puree
- 1 tsp tomato paste
- Salt and black pepper to taste
- Pinch of gari, for garnish
- Spring onions (scallions), sliced, for garnish

1. In a large pot, cook the black-eyed beans in salted water until tender (about 45–60 minutes). Drain and set aside.
2. In a large saucepan, heat the oil over medium heat. Once hot, add the onion and sauté for about 3 minutes until softened.
3. Add the ginger and Scotch bonnet pepper. Sauté for another 2–3 minutes, stirring occasionally.
4. Stir in the cayenne pepper (if using), curry powder and smoked paprika. Cook for another minute to allow the spices to release their flavours.
5. Add the tomatoes, tomato puree and tomato paste to the saucepan. Stir well to combine.
6. Let the mixture simmer on medium heat for about 10 minutes, stirring occasionally, until the tomatoes break down and the sauce thickens.
7. Add the black-eyed beans to the tomato sauce and mix well. Reduce the heat to low and simmer for an additional 20–30 minutes, allowing the flavours to meld. Stir occasionally and adjust seasoning with salt and black pepper to taste.
8. Garnish with gari and spring onions (scallions). Serve the beans hot with a side of fried plantains for a complete meal.

NUTS ABOUT TIGER NUTS

I'm somehow thankful to my body for having zero tolerance for things that are not powered by plants. One day I was on the road with a friend, and he happened to be eating cookies that said "coconut cookies" on the packaging. I assumed they were vegan, so I popped one in my mouth. A few minutes later, I could feel a war raging inside me, and I knew I had eaten something that my body refused to respect or appreciate, and took it to be poison, not food.

Whenever I feed my body vegetables and grains, I have feelings of comfort, satisfaction and inner peace. As I was trying to nurse my lactose-intolerant body after eating a piece of that cookie, which contained cow's milk, my feelings were the opposite.

Being lactose intolerant and wanting to try my best to find a better plant-based milk alternative, I found tiger nuts. Tiger nuts are actually tubers and not nuts; they grow underground and are smaller than most tubers. This healthy food was discovered in ancient Egypt and has been consumed across North and West Africa for years. To be honest with you, had I not decided to go on a plant-based journey, chances are I would never have known that one of the healthiest and tastiest milks I would ever drink would come from tubers.

With its resistant starch fibre content, calcium and protein, it made sense for this delicious milk alternative to be my option of choice. Apart from being perfect to use in teas and coffees or to drink on its own, it's also great in puddings because of its high starch content, as it thickens up when heated to a pudding consistency.

These are the kinds of ingredients that make my life so much easier and mean that I don't miss having dairy as part of my diet.

Koko

SERVES 4

Tiger Nut Milk Pudding

- 200 g (7 oz) tiger nuts
- 330 ml (1⅓ cups) water, divided
- 70 g (½ cup) rice flour
- ¼–½ tsp salt (to taste)
- 75 ml (5 tbsp) agave syrup (or sugar)
- ½ tsp ground cardamom
- Fresh berries or fruit sauce, e.g. passion fruit sauce (optional)

1. Remove any damaged tiger nuts. Rinse the remaining ones thoroughly and soak them in water for several hours or overnight. Avoid soaking them for too long, as they may ferment.
2. After soaking, drain and rinse the tiger nuts again. Place them in a blender with 200 ml (⅔ cup) fresh water. Blend for about 5 minutes until smooth.
3. Place cheesecloth over a metal strainer set over a bowl. Pour the blended mixture into the cheesecloth, then gather the edges and squeeze out as much liquid as possible into the bowl.
4. Open the cheesecloth, pour an additional 130 ml (½ cup) water over the pulp and squeeze again to extract more milk. Discard the leftover pulp.
5. In a medium saucepan, whisk together the rice flour with the tiger nut milk until smooth. Add salt (to taste), the agave syrup and the cardamom. Stir well.
6. Heat the mixture over medium heat, stirring continuously. The pudding will begin to thicken in a few minutes. Once it reaches the desired consistency, remove it from the heat immediately.
7. Pour the pudding into serving glasses or bowls. Place in the fridge to chill and set for at least an hour.
8. Top with fresh berries or a berry sauce of your choice, if desired, before serving.

MY OKRA AWAKENING

Okra wasn't something that was in our household when I was growing up. I remember visiting other homes and seeing people eat okra, and it made my heart sink. I just couldn't understand why anyone would eat or add such a mucilaginous ingredient to their meals. I didn't like how it looked, and its slimy texture simply put me off. I was always hesitant to try it for fear of not being able to swallow it.

One fateful day, in my adult years, I walked past a woman who was selling vegetables on the street. By then I had started my food adventures and for the sake of recipe development and food tasting, I decided to buy some okra from her and try to re-create something with it. Once I plucked up the courage to use it, let's just say that I was pleasantly surprised.

It had a surprisingly nice and almost fatty taste to it. It added texture to any dish and took on flavour quite well. As if that wasn't enough, I discovered that this African vegetable was healthy too. It was through my okra experience that I learnt that we should never discount any ingredient before trying it – as long as it is plant-based. I hope this Ghanaian staple dish, which we call a soup even though it is quite stew-like, makes you appreciate this versatile vegetable more.

Okra Soup

SERVES 3

1 tbsp olive oil

200 g (7 oz) oyster mushrooms, sliced

1 tsp smoked paprika

1 tsp cumin

1 tsp soya sauce

1 tbsp grapeseed oil or African red palm oil

300 g (10½ oz) okra, sliced

Salt to taste

1 large red bell pepper, chopped

2 garlic cloves, minced

1 Scotch bonnet pepper, finely chopped (optional, adjust for heat level)

2 medium tomatoes, chopped

250 ml (1 cup) vegetable stock (or 250 ml/1 cup water with 1 vegetable stock cube)

1. Heat the olive oil in a small saucepan over medium heat. Add the mushrooms, smoked paprika, cumin and soya sauce. Stir-fry until the mushrooms are well caramelised and all the moisture has evaporated (about 5–7 minutes). Remove from heat and set aside.
2. In a separate large saucepan, heat the grapeseed oil over medium heat.
3. Add the okra and stir-fry for 5 minutes. Season with salt. Remove a few cooked okra slices for garnishing later.
4. Add the red bell pepper, garlic and Scotch bonnet pepper to the okra. Stir-fry for another 5 minutes.
5. Stir in the tomatoes and cook for 1 minute.
6. Pour in the vegetable stock, stir and cover the pot with a lid. Allow the soup to simmer for 5–10 minutes until the vegetables are tender.
7. Add the stir-fried mushrooms to the soup and stir to combine. Cover and let it simmer for an additional 3 minutes to allow the flavours to blend.
8. Taste and adjust the seasoning with more salt if necessary.
9. Garnish with the reserved okra slices and serve hot.

WHAT ARE TIGER NUTS?

Tiger nuts are edible tubers that were cultivated in ancient Egypt. They were commonly used for medicinal purposes but were also consumed as food. Because of their insoluble fibre, tiger nuts are easy to digest. They are also rich in iron and vitamin E. Although they were historically grown in Egypt, today they are primarily cultivated in West Africa, where they remain a popular ingredient in both traditional and modern cuisine.

BURKINA FASO

TEN

WELCOME TO THE LAND OF INCORRUPTIBLE PEOPLE

Burkina Faso means the land of incorruptible people, and I fell in love with the country because of one of its former presidents, Thomas Sankara. I watched a documentary about his life, and he was indeed an honourable man. Something that has motivated my journey into revolutionising African indigenous food is what he once said to his people: “Our country produces enough to feed us all. Alas, for lack of organisation, we are forced to beg for food aid. It’s this aid that instils in our spirits the attitude of beggars.” I know I sound like a broken record, but this quote echoes what I have always said and keep saying. Our challenges with food have nothing to do with having enough, they’re about effectively using and preserving the food we produce.

Sankara died before I turned two. In his last speech before his assassination on the 15th of October 1987 he said: “While revolutionaries as individuals can be murdered, you cannot kill ideas.” I was inspired by his revolution. There is no way I can write a book without looking into Burkina Faso. As much as I know very little about its food culture, since I have not been there personally, I have learnt from those who have.

Burkina Faso’s cuisine is similar to that of other West African countries. Though Senegal considers hibiscus tea its national drink, this same flowery and healthy drink is also loved and appreciated by the Burkinabé. It is commonly known as bissap du Burkina Faso. So, as we explore this beautiful country, let’s start with a glass of cold hibiscus tea.

Bissap

SERVES 4

Hibiscus Tea

200 g (1 cup) granulated sugar	250 ml (1 cup) fresh lime juice
400 ml (1⅔ cups) water	Ice cubes
1 medium pineapple, peeled	Fresh mint leaves, for garnish
100 g (3½ oz) dried hibiscus flowers	

1. In a medium saucepan, bring the sugar and half the water to a boil. Stir until the sugar dissolves (about 3 minutes).
2. Cut a few slices from the pineapple and set them aside for the garnish. Cube the rest of the pineapple. Add the pineapple cubes to the syrup, reduce the heat and simmer for 10 minutes to infuse the pineapple flavour.
3. Pour in the rest of the water and add the dried hibiscus flowers. Simmer for an additional 10 minutes.
4. Remove the saucepan from the heat and let the mixture sit for 30 minutes to allow all the flavours to blend.
5. Stir in the lime juice. Cover the mixture and refrigerate for at least 30 minutes to chill.
6. Strain the mixture into an airtight container, discarding the hibiscus flowers and drained pineapple. Chill the tea for another 30 minutes in the fridge.
7. To serve, pour the tea into ice-filled glasses. Garnish each glass with the reserved pineapple slices and mint leaves.

FROM PETALS TO PLATES

Hibiscus flowers could be found everywhere when I was growing up. They came in different colours and were beautiful. We used to call them our "sweet flowers". They had sweet juice in them, and we enjoyed sucking the juice out of the trumpet-shaped flowers. Apart from that, we didn't see hibiscus as anything other than flowers that were there to be looked at. Hibiscus didn't come to mind in the context of drinks or food.

One happy day, I was invited to lunch by a Zambian family, and they gave me some hibiscus tea after the meal. I loved that tea so much! I memorised the name and started looking for it everywhere. I always made sure my budget allowed me to buy it in bulk. One day I decided to google hibiscus flowers to see what they looked like. Oh, how mad I was when I realised that these were the same flowers we used to trample on! The idea of having to budget to pay for something I once had in abundance and didn't appreciate really broke my heart.

After realising that my knowledge of food, especially plant-based food, was so limited that it put me at a disadvantage, I started this journey of learning about food. Knowing that hibiscus has been used across Africa for many generations, both for refreshments and for medicinal purposes, makes me wonder how we got it so wrong in my home country. I went on to look at the various ways in which different African countries enjoy hibiscus. I loved the Burkina Faso way the most, as the addition of pineapple takes this drink (p. 200) to a whole new level. And I have taken it a step further with the delicious dessert here.

Coconut and Cashew Nut Panna Cotta with Hibiscus Compote

SERVES 6

For the panna cotta

- 50 g (1¾ oz) raw cashew nuts, soaked in water for at least 5 hours
- 60 ml (¼ cup) plant milk (such as almond or soya milk)
- ½ pineapple, diced
- 1 tsp agar powder
- 250 ml (1 cup) water
- 300 ml (1¼ cups) coconut milk
- 70 g (⅓ cup) granulated sugar
- 1 tsp vanilla extract
- 1 tbsp arrowroot powder or cornflour (cornstarch)
- 1 tbsp lemon juice

For the hibiscus compote

- 200 g (1 cup) granulated sugar
- 500 ml (2 cups) water, divided, plus a few tablespoons to make a slurry
- 1 medium pineapple, peeled and cut into small cubes
- 100 g (3½ oz) dried hibiscus flowers
- 1 tbsp fresh lime juice
- 1 tbsp arrowroot powder or cornflour (cornstarch)
- 6 fresh mint leaves (optional)

1. To make the panna cotta, combine the soaked cashew nuts, milk and pineapple in a blender. Blend until smooth, then strain the mixture to remove any solids.

2. In a medium saucepan over medium heat, combine the agar powder with 250 ml (1 cup) water. Stir until the agar has dissolved (about 2–3 minutes).

3. Add the coconut milk, sugar, cashew-pineapple mixture, vanilla extract and arrowroot powder. Keep stirring as the mixture thickens (about 5–7 minutes).

4. Stir in the lemon juice, ensuring the mixture is smooth and well combined.

5. Place your serving cups or moulds on a tray. Pour the mixture evenly into each serving cup (about ½ cup per serving). Let the panna cotta cool slightly before covering each cup with clingfilm.

6. Refrigerate the panna cotta for at least 4 hours or overnight to allow it to fully set.

7. To make the compote, bring the sugar and 250 ml (1 cup) water to a boil in a medium saucepan. Stir until the sugar dissolves (about 3 minutes).

8. Add the pineapple cubes and reduce the heat. Simmer for 10 minutes, then add 250 ml (1 cup) water and the dried hibiscus flowers. Simmer for another 10 minutes.

9. Remove from heat and let the mixture sit at room temperature for 30 minutes to infuse. Strain the liquid into another saucepan, discarding the hibiscus flowers and pineapple. Add the lime juice.

10. Return the strained liquid to medium heat. In a small bowl, mix the arrowroot powder with a few tablespoons of water to form a slurry. Add the slurry to the hibiscus tea, stirring continuously until the compote thickens (about 2–3 minutes).

11. Once the compote has cooled, spoon it over the chilled panna cotta. Garnish with mint leaves and serve cold.

IN THE HANDS OF TRADITION

At least twice a month I host African plant-based feasts. One of the highlights during such a feast was when some people put their forks down and ate with their hands. This reminded me of my childhood, as when I was growing up, we mainly ate with our hands. Most countries in Africa serve a food carrier with their soups and stews. For East Africans that would be ugali, injera, kisra or chapati. For West Africans it would be fufu, swallows or tô. In North Africa we have pita bread, msemen or khobz. In southern Africa we have dombolo, roosterkoek or nshima.

I can't imagine eating any of these food carriers using anything other than one's hands. Hands help us create a sensory connection with our food; we feel the texture and temperature of the food before we can even taste it. There is also a belief around Africa that licking fingers during a meal is a sign that the food was delicious. Eating with our hands also helps enhance digestion – as soon as our fingers touch food, the brain is signalled to start preparing the stomach for the digestion process. Nowadays we have forgotten all these elements that bring health and pleasure back into our food experiences.

Part of going back to basics in terms of food was to start with putting my fork down and connecting with my food using my hands. I'm of the view that there is no better way to enjoy good food than through hand-to-mouth eating, as long as it's done using the right hand. I beg you: if you make tô (also known as saghbo) – a dough-based, ugali-like dish from Burkina Faso – please use your hands to eat it.

Tô

SERVES 2

Millet Flour Balls

400 ml (1⅔ cups) water	¼ tsp salt (or to taste)
150 g (1 cup) millet flour	2 tbsp vegan butter

1. In a large saucepan, bring the water to a boil over high heat.
2. Once the water is boiling, slowly whisk in about ¼ of the millet flour (about 40 g), stirring continuously to prevent lumps from forming. Continue stirring for about 5 minutes.
3. Add ¼ tsp salt or more to taste.
4. Reduce the heat to low. Scoop out about ¼ of the thickened mixture and set it aside in a small bowl.
5. Gradually add the remaining flour (in 3 parts) to the pot, stirring vigorously after each addition until the mixture becomes smooth and thick.
6. Stir in the butter until it melts and is well combined. Add the reserved mixture to the pan little by little, stirring continuously, to prevent it from becoming too thick.
7. After 5 minutes of stirring, the mixture should be thick. Cover the pot and let it cook on very low heat for 10 minutes.
8. Remove the pot from the heat. Shape the paste into small balls, sprinkle with additional salt if needed, and serve with your favourite African stew or soup.

SWEET DREAMS

I don't have a sweet tooth, but once in a while I break my own taste bud rules and find myself indulging in something sweet. I have been fascinated by a pastry that was named after a city in southwestern Burkina Faso called Banfora. It must be extremely delicious for it to be named after a whole city! I love the simplicity of this dessert, which is a cross between a pancake and a scone. It looks similar to Welsh cakes, except that it has pineapple in it. This delicious scone-like dessert is cooked on a stovetop instead of being baked in an oven. This is typical for most African desserts; they are usually easy and need minimal tools to achieve the desired results.

When I was a child, we didn't have an oven. We cooked either on a charcoal stove or simple two-burner stove, or with firewood. This wasn't because my family couldn't afford a stove with an oven, it was simply because there seemed to be no need for it, and most homes I knew didn't have one either. It didn't seem like a piece of essential kitchen equipment back then. Although desserts weren't a big thing in our diet, occasionally my mother would bake something for us. She used a charcoal stove and would add burning charcoal to the lid of the pot, while the bottom of the pot rested on a burning charcoal stove. In all honesty, I thought that was a lot of work to make a simple cake!

This explains why desserts such as mandazi in East Africa and Banfora cakes are very popular. They are easy to make and use minimal tools that anyone who cooks can afford. It's this kind of simplicity and affordability I love about African cooking. Anyone who cares to learn can do it.

Banfora Cakes

MAKES 8–10 CAKES

Traditional Pastries Made from Flour and Spices

- 300 g (2½ cups) self-raising flour, plus extra, for dusting
- Pinch of salt
- 100 g (3½ oz) vegan butter, chilled
- 100 g (½ cup) granulated sugar
- 60 g (2¼ oz) chopped canned pineapple, drained
- 2–3 tbsp plant milk (such as soya milk)
- Cinnamon and sugar mixture for sprinkling

1. Sift the flour and salt into a mixing bowl.
2. Cut the butter into small pieces and add it to the flour mixture. Use your fingers to rub the butter into the flour until it resembles fine breadcrumbs.
3. Stir in the sugar and pineapple until evenly distributed.
4. Gradually add the milk to the mixture until a stiff dough forms. If the mixture is too stiff, add a little more milk as needed.
5. Tip the dough onto a lightly floured surface. Knead gently for about a minute, then roll it out to a round disc about 1 cm (½ inch) thick.
6. Use a round cutter (about 10–12 cm/4–5 inches in diameter) to cut out rounds from the dough.
7. Heat a lightly oiled griddle or frying pan over medium-low heat. Fry the rounds for about 3–4 minutes on each side or until they are golden brown. To create steam and cook them evenly, cover the pan with a lid while one side is frying.
8. Once cooked, transfer the cakes to a wire rack to cool. Before serving, sprinkle with a mixture of cinnamon and sugar.

THE FORGOTTEN GRAIN

I learnt about fonio for the first time in 2019 on an American TV show. I was so fascinated hearing about this amazing grain found on African soil. During my research I discovered that even though fonio is possibly one of the oldest grains in Africa, it is not really a staple in any country across Africa, including in West Africa. We have dishes like jollof, which is a staple in most countries in West Africa, but fonio is not even known about. I once drove around Cape Town and visited every West African food store I could think of to try to find fonio and, to my great disappointment, no one even knew what it was.

As Africans we consume so many grains, and most of them are imported and are not originally African. Ironically, we have made these grains part and parcel of our everyday lives, yet what grows around us is being ignored by us and consumed in other parts of the world. I thought it would be a great idea to introduce you to fonio and give you options for how to prepare this beautiful grain.

Fonio

Base Recipe

100 g (½ cup) fonio

1 tsp grapeseed or other vegetable oil

250 ml (1 cup) water

Salt to taste

1. In a large saucepan, combine the fonio and oil.
2. Add the water and stir. Bring to a boil over medium heat. Add salt to taste.
3. Cover the saucepan, reduce the heat to low and simmer for 1 minute.
4. Remove from heat, keeping the pan covered, and let the fonio rest for 3–5 minutes.
5. Fluff the fonio with a fork while still warm.
6. Serve warm or let it cool. Use in grain bowls, salads, soups or smoothies.

Fonio and Baobab Breakfast Smoothie

SERVES 1

50 g (1¾ oz) cooked fonio

1 tbsp baobab powder

½ tsp cinnamon

½ tsp cardamom

½ tsp nutmeg

1 frozen banana, peeled

1 tbsp hemp seeds

1–2 dates (adjust based on desired sweetness)

250 ml (1 cup) plant milk of your choice

Berries or fruit of your choice, to serve

1. In a blender, combine the fonio, baobab powder, cinnamon, cardamom, nutmeg, banana, hemp seeds, dates and milk.

2. Blend the mixture until smooth and creamy.

3. Pour the smoothie into a glass or bowl and top it with your choice of berries.

Fonio and Mango Salad

SERVES 4

- 2 tbsp lime juice
- 1 tsp agave syrup
- 1 garlic clove, minced
- Salt to taste
- 45 ml (3 tbsp) avocado oil
- 100 g (3½ oz) cooked fonio
- 1 bunch parsley leaves, finely chopped
- 1 bunch mint leaves, finely chopped
- 1 ripe mango, peeled, pitted and diced
- 1 small red onion, finely diced
- 100 g (3½ oz) mixed-colour cherry tomatoes, halved
- 1 small cucumber, seeded and diced
- 40 g (1½ oz) lightly roasted sesame seeds

1. In a small bowl, whisk together the lime juice, agave syrup, garlic and salt. Slowly add the avocado oil while whisking to emulsify.

2. In a large bowl, combine the fonio, parsley, mint, mango, red onion, cherry tomatoes and cucumber.

3. Pour the lime dressing over the salad a little at a time, mixing gently.

4. Top the salad with lightly roasted sesame seeds and serve.

Fonio Jollof

SERVES 4

- 3 medium tomatoes
- 3 red bell peppers
- 2 Scotch bonnet peppers (seeds removed for less heat)
- 1 medium onion, chopped
- 2 garlic cloves
- 2 tbsp grapeseed or other vegetable oil
- 1 tbsp tomato paste
- ½ tsp dried thyme
- ½ tsp ground cardamom
- 1 bay leaf
- ½ tsp curry powder
- Salt to taste
- 150 g (5½ oz) dried fonio
- 60 ml (¼ cup) vegetable stock

1. In a blender, combine the tomatoes, red bell peppers, Scotch bonnet peppers, half the onion and the garlic cloves. Blend until smooth and set aside.

2. In a large pot, heat the oil over medium heat. Add the remaining chopped onion and sauté for 3–5 minutes until translucent.

3. Add the tomato paste to the pot and sauté for an additional 5 minutes on low to medium heat.

4. Add the blended tomato and pepper mixture to the pot and cook until thickened and dark red in colour. Stir in the thyme, cardamom, bay leaf, curry powder and salt.

5. Add the fonio and vegetable stock to the pot. Stir well, cover and reduce the heat to low. Allow the fonio to cook for 5 minutes.

6. After 5 minutes, turn off the heat and let the pot sit covered for another 10 minutes without stirring.

7. After resting, remove the bay leaf and fluff the fonio with a fork. Serve with stir fried peppers and chopped cilantro as a garnish, if desired.

CELEBRATING DIVERSITY OF FLAVOURS

I love exploring how countries within Africa interpret the same indigenous food so differently. The first time my Nigerian friend Ada introduced me to yam porridge, as a Rwandan I was sceptical, as I would never have put the words yam and porridge in the same sentence. Lo and behold, there I was, eating a bowl of chopped-up yams in a porridge.

The closest Rwandan dish that resembles this one is what we call imvange (the direct translation is "mixture"). This is a dish where we combine root vegetables, especially potatoes, with beans, another green vegetable and a little palm oil. As for yams, I was only used to eating them in their simplest form as a steamed side dish.

A while back, I came across ragoût d'igname, which is a Burkina Faso version of the dish. When I tried and compared it to what I grew up with and what I had tasted at Ada's home, I would like to believe that Burkina Faso wanted to create something that was in the middle of the two dishes. I guess this was an attempt to keep everyone happy.

Ragoût d'igname is cooked in a tomato sauce similar to the one in the dish I ate in Ada's home. I loved how the yams didn't lose themselves completely in the tomato sauce. This is not one of those comparisons about who does it best – I'm just trying to highlight my favourite. Different methods showcase the beauty of yams retaining their texture and flavour. I know that each country claims to make the best, and they are all right – this is the beauty of life!

While it's important to have our own perspective on life and have grounded convictions, we must also understand that the person next to us has their own way in which they see the world. Even our taste buds are different, and that's okay. Unity in diversity only becomes a thing of beauty when we get to a point where we celebrate our differences, even when it comes to food, without shaming others for doing things differently.

Ragoût d'Igname

SERVES 4

Yam Porridge

- 3 tbsp grapeseed or other vegetable oil
- 1 medium onion, diced
- 3 garlic cloves, minced
- Salt to taste
- 500 g (1 lb 2 oz) mushrooms, sliced
- 3–4 medium-sized tomatoes, diced
- 1 vegetable bouillon cube
- 500 ml (2 cups) vegetable stock
- 1 medium-sized yam, peeled and cubed (about 500 g/1 lb 2 oz)
- Soya sauce to taste
- Handful of spinach, for serving

1. Heat the oil in a saucepan over medium heat. Add the onion and garlic, sprinkle with salt and sauté until the onions become translucent (about 3 minutes).

2. Add the mushrooms to the saucepan and sauté for about 2 minutes, until they start to soften.

3. Stir in the tomatoes and bouillon cube. Let the mixture simmer for about 5 minutes, allowing the flavours to combine.

4. Pour in the vegetable stock and bring the mixture to a boil. Add the yam, reduce the heat to a simmer and cook for about 15 minutes or until the yam is tender. Stir frequently, and if the porridge thickens too much, add more stock or water as needed.

5. For an added touch of colour, add spinach to this dish: wilt a handful of spinach in a separate pan with the remaining oil (1 tbsp).

6. Once the yam is cooked through and the porridge has thickened, stir in the spinach (if using), taste and adjust the seasoning with salt and soya sauce as needed.

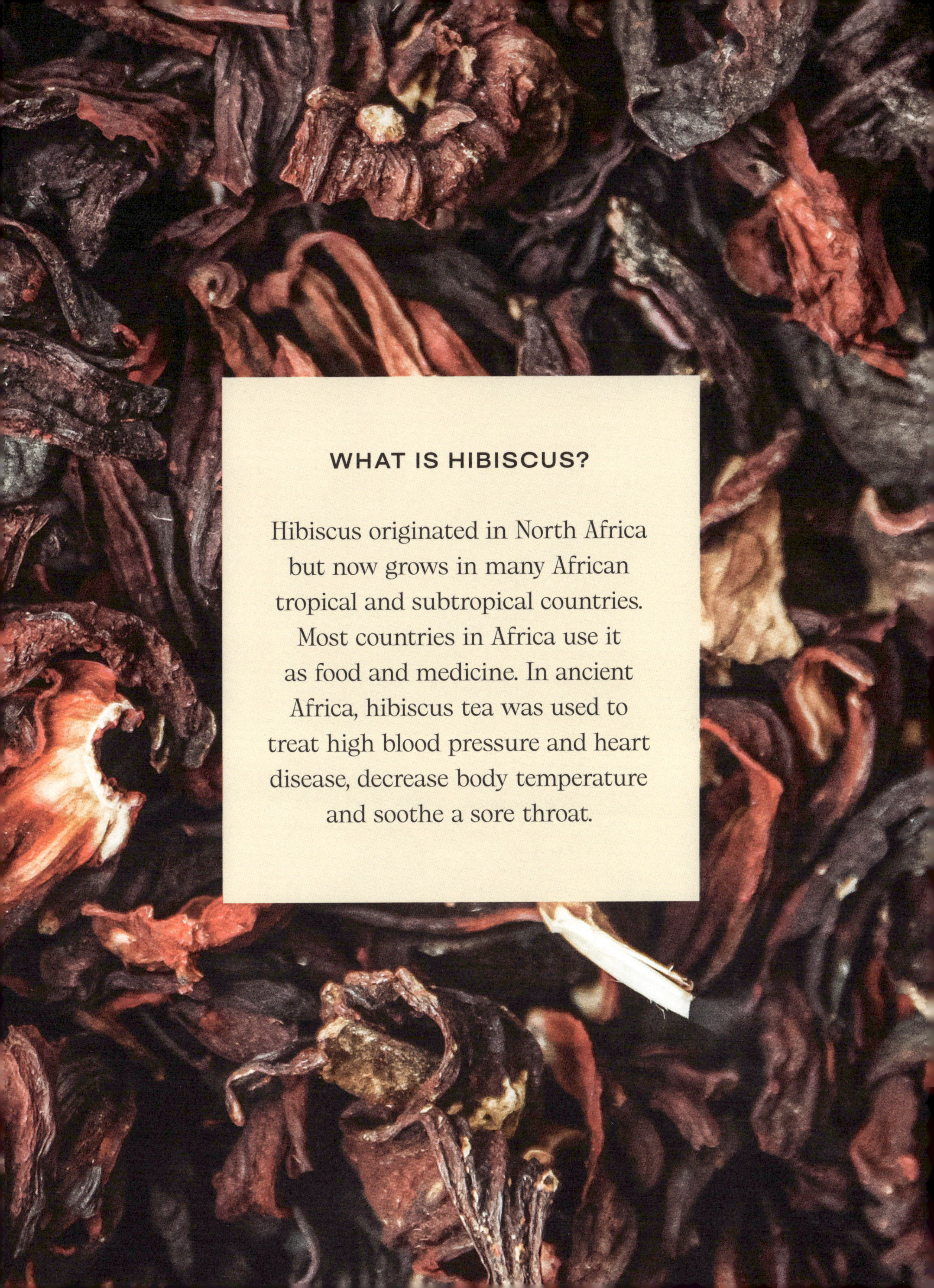

WHAT IS HIBISCUS?

Hibiscus originated in North Africa but now grows in many African tropical and subtropical countries. Most countries in Africa use it as food and medicine. In ancient Africa, hibiscus tea was used to treat high blood pressure and heart disease, decrease body temperature and soothe a sore throat.

MOR OCCO

ELEVEN

A DATE WITH DELICIOUSNESS

When I heard that Morocco is a significant producer of dates, I found myself daydreaming about living there. I've never been there, but I've built a perfect picture of the place in my mind. To me, Morocco is full of colour, warmth and the spice that fills its markets – a kind of magic that reminds me of all the fairy tales I grew up reading.

For those who know how my taste buds work, they're aware that I've always preferred savoury over sweet. But here's a little truth that most people don't know: I have a soft spot for dates. There's always a pack of them in my kitchen. On stressful days, dates are one of the few things, after prayer, that settle me. A quiet comfort. A little moment of stillness.

So, the idea of being surrounded by dates or walking through streets where they're sold in abundance feels like a kind of luxury I could get used to – maybe even a constant "hakuna matata" (no worries) feeling.

Although I haven't made it to Morocco yet, I've read about it and met many people from there who keep feeding my longing to go. When my childhood friend Gilbert went to study there in the early 2000s, I remember taking a taxi to the nearest internet café almost every day, hoping he'd sent me an email. He would paint a picture of Morocco that made me daydream about living there. It hasn't happened yet, but it's definitely made it onto my bucket list. For now, I make my own date syrup and add it to almost everything, just to bring a little sweetness to my day and a touch of magic to the ordinary.

Dibis

MAKES 250 ML (1 CUP)

Date Syrup

- 500 g (1 lb 2 oz) dried pitted dates
- 1 litre (4 cups) water
- Pinch of salt

1. Roughly chop the dates and rinse them thoroughly in a bowl.
2. Add the dates and water to a large saucepan. Bring the mixture to a gentle boil over medium heat. Once it reaches a boil, reduce the heat to low, cover the saucepan and let it simmer for 2 hours.
3. After 2 hours, remove the saucepan from the heat and let the cooked dates cool completely. Once cooled, pour the mixture into a cheesecloth or nut milk bag. Squeeze out as much liquid as possible into a bowl, working in batches to ensure all the juice is extracted.
4. Transfer the strained date juice into a clean saucepan and add a pinch of salt. Bring it to a gentle simmer over low heat. Let it simmer uncovered for about 1 hour, stirring occasionally, until the liquid reduces by half and thickens enough to coat the back of a spoon.
5. Remove the syrup from the heat. As it cools it will continue to thicken, so make sure it doesn't reduce too much while it's simmering.

NOTE:

- Use the date syrup as a natural sweetener for pancakes or ice cream, or in your favourite dishes.

BREAKING TRADITION, ONE PITA AT A TIME

Chapatis have always played a big role in my family's get-togethers. One year I decided to host my mother's birthday at my home. I was fascinated by Moroccan cuisine at the time, and I had learnt all about za'atar and all the amazing flavours from the north, so I decided to make pita bread instead of chapatis for our family get-together. To understand the magnitude of what I was doing, remember that this was not just a get-together, it was the queen's birthday.

I can still see my father looking at the food on the table with shock written all over his face. He asked me if I had changed the style of how I normally made chapatis because my chapatis looked thicker and smaller than our normal ones. I couldn't help but feel very knowledgeable as I took the time to educate my family about this new bread we were about to have instead of chapatis. I told them that we were not having chapatis because we needed to explore other cuisines. I explained to them that pita bread was a Middle Eastern/North African flatbread. However, unlike chapatis, which were unleavened, the pita was leavened with yeast. I watched my father eat my homemade pita bread, and before I knew it, the platter was empty and everyone around the table was giving orders for the next time they visited. Taking baby steps when trying new cuisines can lead us to new beginnings and a new world full of amazing flavours.

Khobz

MAKES 12

Pita Bread

10 g (1/3 oz) instant yeast	700 g (5½ cups) bread flour
550 ml (2⅕ cups) warm water	15 g (½ oz) salt
1 tbsp granulated sugar	60 ml (4 tbsp) olive oil

1. In the bowl of a stand mixer, combine the yeast, water, sugar and 350 g of the flour to form a sponge. Let the sponge rest for 10 minutes until it becomes bubbly.

2. After 10 minutes, add the salt and 45 ml/3 tbsp of the olive oil to the sponge mixture. Gradually add the remaining flour little by little until the dough forms a cohesive ball.

3. Knead the dough on medium speed for about 10 minutes until it becomes smooth, shiny and elastic.

4. Use the remaining olive oil to lightly oil a large bowl. Place the dough in the bowl, rolling it around to coat it with the oil. Cover with a clean towel and let the dough rise in a warm place for about 2 hours or until it doubles in size.

5. After the dough has risen, divide it into 12 equal pieces. Roll each piece into a ball and flatten them into 20 cm (8-inch) rounds. Let the rounds rest for 20 minutes.

6. Just before cooking, roll each round out again to maintain the 20 cm (8-inch) size. Preheat a skillet or pan over medium heat. Place a pita in the pan and cook for 3–5 minutes on each side until puffed and golden. Repeat with the remaining dough rounds.

7. After cooking, wrap the pitas in a clean dish towel and place them in a plastic bag to keep them soft and pliable. Serve with chopped herbs and chilli flakes.

A LEGUME REVOLUTION

It feels as though some foods only came into existence once I started a plant-based lifestyle. Fifteen years ago, I had never heard of half the foods I eat today. I don't think I would have known what sumac was had I not started this beautiful adventure of plant-based living. I'm thankful for this lifestyle that introduced me to such a variety of foods. I now keep sumac and chickpeas as a pantry staple. Who would have thought?

I remember the first time I ate hummus. I swear I felt as though I was on another planet. I can vividly recall the combination, from the blended creamy chickpeas with tahini to the freshness of lemon and the warmth of cumin. Without a shadow of a doubt, I knew this was a keeper. I am married to this beautiful dip and I have no thoughts of divorce. It has truly brought so many colours into my world – both figuratively and literally. Hummus not only added vibrancy to my culinary experience, it also added colour by means of the vegetables and spices I used while experimenting with this recipe. Hummus has also helped me realise that when we are intentional in our cooking, it forces us to get out of our comfort zone in order to remain true to the call. I have found a way to add colour and flavour to this already perfect treat without taking away from its Middle Eastern heritage.

Hummus Bi Tahina

Chickpeas and Tahini Dip

MAKES 500 G (2 CUPS), SERVING ABOUT 4–6

- 300 g (10½ oz) dried split chickpeas (or whole chickpeas, if preferred)
- 500 ml (2 cups) water, for boiling
- ¾ tsp fine sea salt, plus extra for boiling the chickpeas
- 4 medium garlic cloves, with skins on, smashed
- 2 tbsp extra-virgin olive oil, plus extra to drizzle
- 40 g (1½ oz) good-quality tahini
- ½ tsp ground cumin
- Juice of 1 lemon (about 2–3 tbsp)
- 2–4 tbsp cold water (or more, as needed)
- Fresh parsley, chopped
- Handful of cherry tomatoes, halved
- Ground sumac (optional)

1. Soak the chickpeas in water for at least 5 hours. After soaking, rinse and drain them.

2. In a pot, add the water, salt and chickpeas. Bring to a boil and cook for about 30 minutes until the chickpeas are soft. (Split chickpeas cook faster than whole ones and make smoother hummus because they lack skins.)

3. While the chickpeas are cooking, preheat the oven to 180 °C (350 °F). Place the garlic cloves in a small oven dish, drizzle with olive oil and roast for about 10 minutes, until softened. Be careful not to burn them. Allow both the chickpeas and garlic to cool completely.

4. Once cooled, peel the garlic and transfer it to a food processor along with the cooked chickpeas, 2 tbsp olive oil, tahini, cumin, lemon juice and ¾ tsp salt. Puree until smooth, stopping halfway to scrape down the sides of the bowl.

5. If the hummus is too thick, add cold water a spoonful at a time and continue blending until the desired smooth consistency is reached. Taste and adjust seasoning with more salt, cumin or lemon juice if needed.

6. Transfer the hummus to a bowl and garnish with a drizzle of olive oil, parsley, cherry tomatoes and a sprinkle of sumac (if using). Serve immediately with crisp bread slices or crackers or store in an airtight container in the fridge for up to a week.

FLAVOURS OF THE EARTH

Because I come from Rwanda, I fully understand the idea of cooking in clay pots. When I was growing up, I heard that food cooked in an old clay pot tasted much better than food cooked in steel or aluminium pots. Apparently the clay pot brings you closer to the ground from which your food is taken and adds flavour.

Unfortunately, over the years I have had less and less access to the kind of clay pots I used to see in my grandmother's kitchen. By the time I became a seasoned cook, I had lost all access to such luxury. When I saw a tagine (a Moroccan traditional cooking pot made of clay) in Cape Town, where I live, I knew I wanted to own one regardless of how much it cost. I knew that it was the closest I might get to the clay pots in my grandmother's kitchen, so it was worth the investment.

In honour of this masterpiece, and as my way of celebrating my first tagine, I needed to prepare something Moroccan in it.

Roasted vegetables with chickpeas in my new tagine seemed like the best way to start. Let's just say that this recipe has become one of my favourites.

NOTES:

- You can use fresh coriander or mint leaves to garnish the tagine.
- Serve it hot with cooked fonio (p. 208) or your preferred grain such as couscous or quinoa.

Tajine Bil Khodar

SERVES 4 AS A MAIN DISH

Slow-cooked Vegetable Stew

- 1 medium eggplant (aubergine), cut into chunks
- 1 tsp sea salt
- 2 medium carrots, quartered
- ½ red bell pepper, cut into chunks
- ½ green bell pepper, cut into chunks
- ½ yellow bell pepper, cut into chunks
- 100 g (3½ oz) butternut squash, peeled and diced
- 1 large potato, cut into chunks
- 1 tbsp olive oil, plus extra to drizzle
- ½ tsp dried rosemary
- 1 can (425 g/15 oz) diced tomatoes
- 250 ml (1 cup) vegetable stock
- 1 tsp tomato paste
- 1 tsp date syrup (p. 224, or substitute with maple syrup)
- 4 garlic cloves, peeled and left whole
- 4 button mushrooms, quartered
- ½ medium onion, roughly chopped
- ½ tsp ground cumin
- ½ tsp ground coriander
- ½ tsp ground turmeric
- 1 can (425 g/15 oz) chickpeas, drained and rinsed
- Fresh mint, for garnish

1. Place the eggplant in a bowl, sprinkle with salt and let it sit for 20 minutes to draw out the bitterness. Rinse off the salt thoroughly and pat dry with paper towels.

2. Preheat the oven to 200 °C (400 °F). In a large bowl, toss the eggplant, carrots, red, green and yellow bell peppers, butternut and potato with the olive oil and dried rosemary. Spread the vegetables on a baking tray and roast for 20 minutes or until they are lightly browned and tender.

3. In a small bowl, mix the tomatoes, vegetable stock, tomato paste and date syrup. Set aside to let the flavours blend.

4. While the vegetables are roasting, heat a tagine or deep pan over medium heat. Add a drizzle of olive oil, then sauté the garlic, mushrooms and onion for 5–10 minutes, until the garlic and onion start to brown slightly.

5. Stir in the cumin, coriander and turmeric. Add the chickpeas and cook for another 2–3 minutes, stirring to coat the chickpeas in the spices.

6. Once the roasted vegetables are ready, add them to the tagine along with the tomato sauce mixture. Stir to combine, then cover and simmer for 15–20 minutes until all the vegetables are tender and the sauce has thickened.

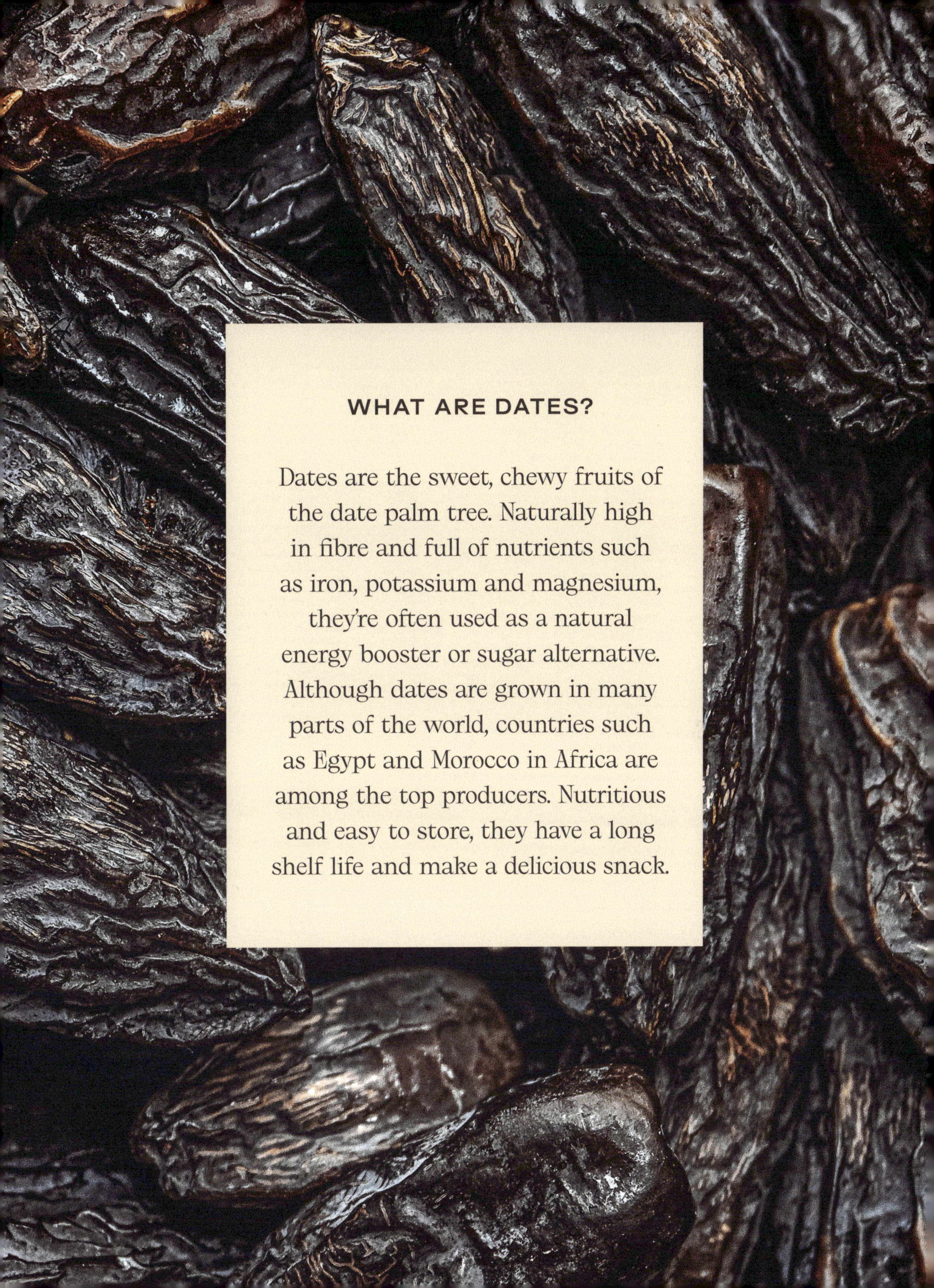

WHAT ARE DATES?

Dates are the sweet, chewy fruits of the date palm tree. Naturally high in fibre and full of nutrients such as iron, potassium and magnesium, they're often used as a natural energy booster or sugar alternative. Although dates are grown in many parts of the world, countries such as Egypt and Morocco in Africa are among the top producers. Nutritious and easy to store, they have a long shelf life and make a delicious snack.

EGYPT

TWELVE

FROM CAPE TO CAIRO

Food is our greatest connector. In 2021 I was asked to do a feature on East African cuisine by South Africa's *Fresh Living* magazine for its African month issue. What I didn't realise is that through that experience I would meet other chefs from all over Africa who were also featured and that they would become my foodie buddies.

When the magazine was published, I got to meet Mary Fawzy, who is a food and culture writer and recipe developer. I have always been fascinated by Egypt's rich history and cuisine. Meeting Mary was an opportunity to learn that I was not going to let pass me by. When I asked Mary to host an Egyptian plant-based cooking class with me at Makers Landing at the V&A Waterfront in Cape Town, I was so happy when she gladly agreed to do it. That class was such a ride and it was an experience I wish I could have bottled! Nevertheless, the dishes we prepared together will always be there to take me back to that experience and to transport me straight from Cape to Cairo. In honour of Mary, I decided to re-create my own twist on her favourite recipe.

Torshi Lift

Egyptian Purple Pickled Turnips

MAKES ABOUT 1 LITRE (ABOUT 4 CUPS)

- 500 ml (2 cups) water
- 470 ml (scant 2 cups) white vinegar
- 1 tbsp fennel seeds
- 1 tbsp coriander seeds
- 40 g (1½ oz) good-quality salt (e.g. pink Himalayan salt)
- 700 g (1½ lb) fresh, firm turnips, peeled and cut into 1 cm (½-inch) sticks or slices
- 1 large red beetroot, peeled and cut into 1 cm (½-inch) sticks or slices
- 3 garlic cloves, peeled and sliced
- Bay leaves (one for each jar)

1. In a saucepan, combine the water, vinegar, fennel seeds, coriander seeds and salt. Bring the mixture to a boil over medium heat. Once it boils, reduce the heat to low, cover and simmer for 10 minutes to infuse the flavours. Remove from heat and let the brine cool completely.

2. In sterilised jars, layer the turnips, beetroot and garlic. Add a bay leaf to each jar for extra flavour.

3. Pour the cooled brine over the vegetables in the jars using a sieve, making sure the turnips and beetroot are fully submerged. Distribute the fennel and coriander seeds from the brine more or less evenly among the jars.

4. Screw the lids on tightly and place the jars in a cool, dark place for 1 week to allow the pickling and fermentation process to take place.

5. After 1 week, transfer the jars to the fridge. The pickled turnips will continue to develop flavour over time and are best consumed within 2 months.

THE POWER OF PEANUTS

If there is one trending theme in all African countries when it comes to food, it's the love of peanuts. Oh boy, do we love our peanuts! There is no country in Africa that doesn't have at least one popular dish with them in it. I would like to take this moment to vote for peanuts, the ultimate African ingredient. As a matter of fact, I think African peanut sauce deserves recognition as a "mother sauce" in its own right, much like the classic French mother sauces, and should be included in culinary education to represent Africa's rich culinary tradition.

I can't imagine a better ingredient than peanuts that Africa as a whole would relate to. As Mary and I were going through the list of all the ingredients for the Egyptian cooking class in Cape Town and I saw peanuts were on the list, my heart smiled. I feel like there should be a law that states that no plant-based meal should be put together without a touch of peanuts. The following recipe brings everything together perfectly.

Dukkah

SERVES 10–12

Blend of Roasted Nuts, Seeds and Spices

- 100 g (3½ oz) peanuts
- 2 tsp toasted sesame seeds
- 1 tsp ground cumin
- 1 tsp ground coriander
- 1 tsp nigella seeds (also known as black cumin)
- ½ tsp salt (or to taste)

1. Preheat the oven to 180 °C (350 °F). Place the peanuts on a baking tray and toast them for 5–7 minutes or until fragrant. Allow them to cool completely.
2. Grind the peanuts into a coarse powder using a pestle and mortar, food processor or spice grinder.
3. In a bowl, combine the peanuts, sesame seeds, cumin, coriander, nigella seeds and salt.
4. Mix well until all the ingredients are evenly blended.
5. Store the dukkah spice blend in an airtight container at room temperature for up to 1 month or refrigerate for a longer shelf life.

NOTES:

- Serve with salads, wraps or soups; use as a dip; mix with olive oil and serve with crusty bread for a classic Egyptian snack; or use as a seasoning for vegetables.
- Add other spices or herbs such as cinnamon, cardamom or thyme to create unique flavour profiles.
- Experiment with different types of nuts or seeds, such as almonds or pumpkin seeds.

A BITTER BATTLE WITH EGGPLANTS

I never used to be a lover of eggplants. That's probably because for a long time I didn't know how to cook them properly and they always ended up being bitter. I have had enough bitter moments in my life, and the last place I want to experience bitterness is in my mouth.

My relationship with eggplants changed a couple of years ago, when I learnt a great tip from David Mwenze, a chef I admire. He mentioned the importance of choosing the right eggplants. Choose young, firm eggplants with glossy, unblemished skin and a vibrant green stem. These tend to have fewer seeds and a milder flavour, without the bitterness that can develop as the fruit matures. He also suggested that before using an eggplant, you should salt it to remove excess water, which causes the bitterness. Make sure you rinse off the salt and pat the eggplant dry with paper towels before you continue with the preparation. I have faithfully been using this method to prepare my eggplants ever since.

I was so excited when I tried Egyptian marinated eggplants, as I was able to enjoy the delicious eggplant taste without any bitterness.

Betingan Bil Zeit

SERVES 6

Marinated Eggplant (Aubergine)

- 6 medium eggplants (aubergines), sliced into 1 cm (1/2 inch) thick rounds
- Salt to coat
- 150 ml (2/3 cup) olive oil
- 150 ml (2/3 cup) red grape vinegar
- 2 garlic cloves, minced
- 2 tbsp agave syrup (optional)
- Oil for frying (e.g. sunflower oil)

1. Place eggplant slices in a pot and sprinkle with salt to coat. Let them rest for 30 minutes to draw out the bitterness.

2. Rinse the eggplant slices thoroughly under cold running water. Pat dry with paper towels to remove excess moisture.

3. In a bowl, whisk together the olive oil, red grape vinegar, garlic and agave syrup (if using).

4. Heat the frying oil in a pan over high heat. Fry the eggplant slices for 3 minutes on each side or until soft and golden brown. Remove from oil and place on paper towels to drain excess oil.

5. In a sterilised, sealable container, arrange the fried eggplant slices. Pour the marinade over the aubergine slices, ensuring they're fully coated. Seal container and refrigerate.

6. The eggplant is ready to serve after 15 minutes. Store refrigerated for up to 2 weeks.

NOTES:

- Adjust the amount of garlic and agave syrup to taste.
- Add herbs such as basil, oregano or thyme to the marinade for extra flavour.
- Use as a side dish, a topping for sandwiches or an addition to salads.

FLAVOURFUL FALAFEL

One of the many gems of knowledge that Mary shared with us during our cooking class was the origin of falafel. According to Mary, and with research to prove it, falafel's origin comes from the Coptic culture. Coptic is what the Egyptian nation was before the Arab conquest of Egypt. Today it's known as the word for Egyptian Christians, who make up 10% of the population. Mary also mentioned that there are so many vegan foods that come from the Coptic heritage because the Copts do vegan fasts for about 200 days of the year. Some of these fasts happen before Easter, Christmas and feasts for various saints.

We also learnt that falafel's direct meaning is "full of beans". What I loved about the Egyptian cooking class was that Mary empowered us to be creative while making falafel. She told us how, when she was growing up in Zambia, they couldn't get broad beans (fava beans), which are usually used to make falafel. They had to find a replacement and that's how her mother started using green split peas – and they never looked back.

This spoke to me, as I refuse to be limited by the inaccessibility of ingredients when making a dish. Chances are there are already 10 ingredients out there that can replace the one you can't get hold of.

Green Split Pea Falafel

MAKES ABOUT 25–30, SERVING 4–6 PEOPLE AS A MAIN DISH

Deep-fried Patties Seasoned with Herbs and Spices

- 500 g (1 lb 2 oz) dried green split peas
- 1 medium yellow or brown onion
- 8 garlic cloves, peeled
- 40 g (1½ oz) fresh dill
- 40 g (1½ oz) fresh coriander (cilantro)
- 20 g (¾ oz) fresh parsley
- 1 tbsp baking powder
- 3 tsp fine sea salt
- 1 tsp ground cumin
- 1 tsp ground coriander
- Handful of sesame seeds
- Oil for frying (e.g. sunflower oil)

1. Rinse the split peas and soak in water (at least 2 cm/1 inch deep) overnight or for up to 12 hours.
2. Drain and pat dry with a clean kitchen towel.
3. Finely chop the onion and garlic in a food processor.
4. Add the dill, fresh coriander and parsley; blend until finely chopped.
5. Add the split peas to the herb mixture and blend to a coarse paste.
6. Transfer the mixture to a bowl and add the baking powder, salt, cumin and ground coriander. Mix well by hand.
7. Let the mixture rest for 30 minutes at room temperature. Shape into falafel or meatball shapes, then flatten slightly into round discs.
8. Dip each falafel in sesame seeds, coating the whole surface.
9. Heat oil in a pan (at least a third full) over high heat. Carefully add the falafel and reduce the heat to medium.
10. Cook until golden brown (2–3 minutes per side).
11. Remove with a slotted spoon and drain excess oil on paper towels. Serve with a dip such as Hummus Bi Tahina (p. 229).

NOTES:

- Adjust seasoning to taste.
- Add other herbs or spices, such as ginger root, for unique flavours.
- Bake the falafel instead of frying for a healthier option (190 °C/375 °F, 20–25 minutes).
- Serve in pita bread with tahini sauce, lettuce and tomatoes.

CAROB UNCOVERED

When I organised the Egyptian cooking class at Makers Landing, I knew it would be special; however, I didn't realise just how much heart Mary, our guest chef, would bring with her. She arrived at the Demo Kitchen (which was the space used for cooking classes at Makers Landing) that morning like a burst of sunshine, carrying trays of basbousa (a sweet, golden semolina cake) and a large bottle of carob juice for everyone to share.

It seemed like a simple gesture, yet it filled the room with warmth before we had even begun cooking. I remember pouring myself a small cup of her homemade carob juice out of curiosity, only to find myself returning for more again and again. It was sweet, earthy and refreshing – perfect for that day's weather. We grew up in a Seventh Day Adventist home, where we were encouraged to avoid caffeine, so carob powder often replaced cocoa powder whenever we made chocolate cake. That was the extent of my relationship with carob: just an ingredient used as a substitute, nothing more.

I had no idea it could be transformed into such a refreshing, vibrant drink, standing on its own. That day, thanks to Mary's gift, I saw carob in a whole new light.

Kharroub

Egyptian Carob Juice

MAKES ABOUT 500 ML (2 CUPS), SERVING 2–4

150 g (3/4 cup) granulated sugar, plus extra to taste

250 ml (1 cup) cold water, plus extra if needed

250 ml (1 cup) hot water

60 g (2 1/4 oz) carob powder

Fresh mint leaves, for garnish

1. Combine the sugar and cold water in a saucepan. Heat over low heat, stirring with a metal spoon until the sugar dissolves. Stop stirring and increase the heat to medium.
2. Bring the syrup to a boil; cook for 5 minutes or until the edges start to caramelise.
3. Whisk the hot water and carob powder in a small bowl until smooth.
4. Pour the carob mixture into the caramel saucepan and whisk well. Add more cold water to achieve desired juice consistency. Taste and adjust sweetness level; add more sugar if needed.
5. Set aside to cool. Transfer the cooled juice to a jar and refrigerate.
6. Serve chilled.

NOTES:

- Add flavourings such as vanilla or cinnamon.
- Experiment with different carob powder brands.

WHAT IS CAROB?

Carob beans, also known as locust beans, are found in the pods of carob trees that trace their origins back to the Mediterranean region. Carob is sweet in taste. It has a nutty chocolate flavour and is rich in fibre and antioxidants.

SAVOURING THE JOURNEY: FINDING MY VOICE IN EVERY BITE

There is a saying that you are what you eat. With this book as my witness, what I eat is part of what shapes me. As an African, on every page of the life I have lived, food has not only been a source of nourishment, it has also been the very lens I use to see and connect to the world around me.

There have been very few things in my life that have managed to stir my emotions the way food does. Through food, I remain connected to my African, and specifically Rwandan, roots. Through food, I have managed to show affection to those around me by simply offering them a home-cooked meal made with love. Through food, I have met and connected with strangers who have become family. It was also through food that I found a solace for my broken heart when life disappointed me. It's through food that I am now making my living. It is through food that I gained the courage to open my heart on these pages and invite you into my small and humble world.

I have indeed found my identity and my calling, all wrapped up in food.

INDEX

N

O

P

R

S

T

U

V

W

X/Y/Z

ABOUT THE AUTHOR

Jane Nshuti is a chef and plant-based food educator who was born in Rwanda and raised across several African countries. With a deep commitment to African food traditions, she reimagines indigenous recipes to promote wellness and celebrate African heritage. Her culinary journey began in the refugee camps of the Democratic Republic of Congo, where limited resources sparked her resilience and creativity. Today, Jane is a recognised advocate for plant-based African ingredients, sharing her knowledge through workshops, speaking engagements and the Migrating Home tasting series. Her work embodies a decolonised approach to African cuisine, emphasising cultural identity, food security and community empowerment. As a passionate storyteller and educator, Jane connects audiences across Africa and beyond with the richness of African flavours and the cultural significance embedded in every dish.

THANK-YOUS

This book represents a journey shaped by resilience and an enduring love of African culture. I want to thank my family for their unwavering support through every chapter of my life, from our early days in Rwanda to building a life across Africa.

To my siblings, Charlotte, Bernard, Leonard, Ngema, Jacques, Olivia, Justine and Phoebe, your strength and commitment are the foundation of everything I do.

To my uncle Jotham (who everybody calls Shamba and who became my father) and my aunt Jacqueline (who became my mother), who offered stability and the chance at a fresh start for my brother and me, thank you for your kindness and guidance through difficult times.

To Fritz, who believed in this book and committed to see it come to life just as I did.

To my friend Khona, for being my forever cheerleader and support system, and a committed taster.

To Livhuwani, for bringing each dish to life through your photography skills.

To my husband, Irenee, for caring for our children while I devoted myself to this project. And to my children, Hirwa and Aliane, you are my constant inspiration and motivation to contribute positively to the world you will one day inherit.

I am also deeply grateful to the communities and mentors who have influenced my culinary journey. From neighbours who shared their meals with me and friends who shared their African food journeys with me to the mentors and colleagues in the food industry who helped shape my skills, each of you has left a lasting mark on my heart.

Special thanks to Bertha House, Food Dialogue (Food Indaba), The Plant Powered Show and the Makers Landing Incubator Programme. These platforms allowed me to share my passion for African plant-based cuisine and to spread a message of food as culture, history and healing. Their support has empowered me to educate and inspire others to connect with their African heritage.

Finally, to the readers of this book, thank you. May this work inspire you to explore and celebrate the rich tapestry of African cuisine...

A member of Penguin Random House Verlagsgruppe GmbH
Neumarkter Strasse 28 · 81673 Munich

produktsicherheit@penguinrandomhouse.de

(The above information is mandatory information according to GPSR and should be used for all queries relating to the safety of our books.)

Library of Congress Control Number is available; a CIP catalogue record for this book is available from the British Library.

Text: Jane Nshuti
Photography, art direction and food styling: Livhuwani Ravele
Design and illustration: Emma Wells, Studio Nic+Lou

Editorial direction: Claudia Schönecker
Project management: Veronika Brandt
Copy-editing: Paula Hepburn-Brown
Production management: Martina Effaga
Separations: Reproline Mediateam, Munich
Printing and binding: Mohn Media Mohndruck GmbH, Gütersloh

Penguin Random House Verlagsgruppe FSC® N001967

Printed in Germany

ISBN 978-3-7913-9167-0

www.prestel.com